D1882669

A PICTURE STORY-BOOK OF INDIAN HISTORY

Owing to the antiquity and rarity of this book, certain pages are regrettably absent, and readability is compromised due to the blurring of the original text. If you possess any insights regarding the availability of these missing sections, kindly inform us. Your assistance is crucial in ensuring the completion of this significant work for the benefit of future generations.

A PICTURE STORY-BOOK OF INDIAN HISTORY

GABRIELLE FESTING

GYAN

Published by

Gyan Publishing House
5, Ansari Road
Daryaganj, New Delhi-110002
Phone: 011-47034999, 9811692060
E-mail: books@gyanbooks.com

Distribution Network
gyanbooks.com
India, USA, Canada, UK, Australia

© Publisher

All rights reserved. No part of this work may be reproduced, stored, adapted, or transmitted in any form or by any means, electronic, mechanical, photocopying, micro-filming, recording or otherwise, or translated in any language, without the prior written permission of the copyright owner and the publisher.

ISBN: 978-93-6920-033-7 (PB)

First Published, 1900

2nd Impression 2025

Printed at: Gyan Press, Delhi.

The book is sold subject to the condition that it shall not, by way of trade or otherwise, be lent, resold, hired out, or otherwise circulated without the prior publisher's written consent.

A PICTURE STORY-BOOK OF INDIAN HISTORY
Author: GABRIELLE FESTING

A PICTURE STORY-BOOK OF INDIAN HISTORY

KING GEORGE V: EMPEROR OF INDIA.

Photo. W. and D. Downey, London.

A PICTURE STORY-BOOK OF INDIAN HISTORY

BY

GABRIELLE FESTING

AUTHOR OF "FROM THE LAND OF PRINCES," "WHEN KINGS RODE TO DELHI," "STRANGERS WITHIN THE GATES," ETC., ETC.

WITH OVER ONE HUNDRED ILLUSTRATIONS

BOMBAY

K. & J. COOPER

EDUCATIONAL PUBLISHERS

TO

G., N., & D.

AND

TO ALL CHILDREN WHO MAY READ THIS BOOK.

Some of you may want to know whether these stories from Indian History are all true. There is truth in all of them; but in some of the earlier stories it has been twisted, or else something has been added to it.

Some people explain the story of Rama and Sita by saying that the Rakshasas were really a hostile tribe who stole Sita away and that the monkeys who helped Rama to bring her back were a race of little men who lived in the forests—like the Bhils. We know of Asoka's reign and his good laws, through the inscriptions on the pillars at Allahabad, and Delhi, and elsewhere; but the story about his mother is a tradition which may or may not be true.

We cannot say that all the details in the legend of St. Thomas really happened, but the Christian Church from the very earliest times has had a tradition that he preached and suffered martyrdom in India.

Rana Hamir may not really have had to recover his father's sword from the witches, but he recovered his father's kingdom by his bravery and steadfastness, and the story of the sword may be a sort of allegory of his real struggles with his enemies. The sword, at any rate, really was treasured by the Ranas of Chitor for many generations.

After writing the story of Akbar, I went to hear a lecture from a very learned man, who was quite sure that Akbar really had cut off Himu's head. But as other learned people for many years have said that he did not, I have not altered the story.

If you like these stories, you must remember that they are only a beginning; they were written in the hope that some of you, after reading them would go on to the real books on Indian history, such as those written by Mr. Keene, or Sir George Forrest, or

Mr. Stanley Lane-Poole. This little book may be like a pathway, that leads you to a beautiful garden. But you must not stay on the pathway; you must go on, into the garden, and see what you can find for yourselves.

MODEL OF STONE CHARIOT.

Negative: Archæological Survey.

CONTENTS.

PART I.

LEGENDS OF EARLY INDIA.

PART II.

THE MUSLIM INVASION.

PART III.

STORIES OF THE SULTANS OF DELHI.

PART IV.

THE GREAT DAYS OF THE MOGHUL EMPIRE.

PART V.

THE DECLINE OF THE MOGHUL EMPIRE.

PART VI.

THE DOWNFALL OF THE MOGHUL EMPIRE.

A WATCH TOWER.

Negative: Archæological Survey.

LIST OF ILLUSTRATIONS.

Figs. 19, 20, 23, 26, 27, 34, 39, 40, 45, 49, 55, 59, 63, 67, 73, 74, 80, 87 and 91 are reproduced from photographs by Messrs. Johnston and Hoffmann, Calcutta, and Figs. 37, 42, 47, 56, 60, 65, 69, 81, 88, 95, 101 and 102 from photographs by Messrs. Bourne and Shepherd, India. The majority of the other illustrations are reproduced from photographs kindly oupplied by the Archæological Survey of India, the Trustees of the Victoria Memorial Section, Indian Museum, and the India Office. The Publishers' grateful thanks are also duė to the Maharaja of Bobbili for Fig. 93.

CANNON BALL

FOUND ON THE BATTLEFIELD OF PANIPAT.

PART I.

LEGENDS OF EARLY INDIA.

STORIES OF RAMA AND SITA.

1. THE BOW OF SIVA.
2. THE ENCHANTED DEER.
3. THE ARMY OF MONKEYS.

4. THE GOOD EMPEROR ASOKA.
   (ASOKA DIED 231 B. C.)

5. THE PALACE BUILT BY ST. THOMAS.
   (ABOUT A. D. 45.)

THE BOW OF SIVA.

"Rama took it in his hands, and bent it till it sprang asunder."

From a painting by Ravi Varma.

1. THE BOW OF SIVA.

Once upon a time, a Raja had many sons, and he loved Rama best of them all.

When Rama was still a boy, while shooting with a bow belonging to one of his companions, he broke it. "Ah," said the other boy, "it is easy for you to break my bow; you should go to the Court of Raja Janaka, and try the bow of Siva which he keeps. He has promised his daughter Sita as a wife to the archer who can bend it."

Now Janaka's daughter was fairest of all women, and she was called Sita ("a furrow") because she was born of no earthly mother, but had sprung from the earth when Janaka was ploughing.

So Rama took his favourite brother, Lakshman, with him, and they travelled to the Court of Janaka, where he asked leave to try the bow of Siva.

This bow was so large and heavy that it had to be dragged upon an eight-wheeled cart; Rama took it in his hands, and bent it till it sprang asunder.

The whole Court were so overjoyed that every one, except Janaka himself, turned head over heels. Rama was married to the beautiful Sita, and Lakshman was married to one of her sisters, with great pomp and ceremony.

When the wedding festivities were over, the brothers took their brides to their own home, and their father was so delighted that he promised to leave his kingdom to Rama when he died.

But Rama had a stepmother who was jealous of him, and wanted her own son to have the kingdom, and she gave the old Raja no peace till he consented to do as she wished. Nor was she content with this, but for fear that Rama should change his father's mind again, she wrought with cunning words and with false tales, until the old Raja consented to banish his dear son from the kingdom for ten years.

Rama, like a dutiful son, did not dispute his father's will. He was greatly beloved by his father's people, and when on the appointed day they saw him go through the streets with Lakshman and Sita, who preferred wandering over the world in his company to living in a palace without him, they wailed and

THE WEDDING OF RAMA AND SITA.

wept until their tears laid the dust that had been raised by the wheels of the chariots. The three had cast aside their royal robes and jewels, and put on garments woven from the bark of trees. Out of all their possessions they took with them nothing but the armour and weapons of the two princes, a basket, and a hoe.

They had not gone very far before they were overtaken by Rama's half-brother, the son of the wicked step-mother. The old Raja's heart had broken at parting from Rama, and he had fallen dead; the unkind Rani, at once sent word to her son to take the kingdom for himself. But he reproached her bitterly for her wickedness, and set forth to find Rama and bring him back to reign.

But Rama would not come. "Though my father is dead, I will not disobey him," he said; "he banished me for ten years. I cannot return before those ten years are over."

So the good half-brother went home, sadly, to govern as Rama's regent, and Rama, Lakshman, and Sita wandered away into the jungles.

2. THE ENCHANTED DEER.

After straying up and down for some time, the brothers built a little hut, and lived in it with Sita, among the trees and flowers and wild animals.

Now in the city of Lanka, in the island of Ceylon, lived the terrible Ravana, monarch of the Rakshasas (ogres). Having heard of Sita's beauty, he coveted her for his wife. Not daring to attempt taking her by force from such a renowned warrior as Rama, he determined to get possession of her by craft, with the help of his magical powers.

One day, a deer ran past the hut. Its hide was of gold spotted with silver, its feet were of silver and its horns were covered with jewels. Directly Sita beheld it, she implored Rama to get it for her. Accordingly, he seized his bow and arrows, and ran after it, bidding Lakshman to guard Sita until his return.

For a long time, Rama followed the deer, but though fleet of foot, he could not overtake it. Then he sent an arrow from his bow, which struck it, and as it fell, it sighed "Ah Rama! Ah Sita!" in tones of piteous sadness. The wind carried the sigh through the jungle, till its echo reached the hut where Sita and Lakshman waited.

Sita cried, "Surely, that is the voice of my lord! Some evil has overtaken him. Fly to his help."

At first Lakshman refused to go, urging that Rama had charged him to stay with Sita. Then she upbraided him, vowing that he must be jealous of his brother, if he sat still when Rama called for help, and Lakshman yielded, and hurried away.

While Sita was alone within the hut, there came to the door a man in the dress of a hermit, who seemed spent with hunger and weariness. Sita, as was fitting, brought him food and water, thinking him to be some holy man who was leading a solitary life in the jungle. Great was her horror when he revealed himself to be none other than Ravana.

"Come with me," he told her, "and all Lanka shall be yours, and you shall have five thousand handmaidens to wait upon you."

SITA AND THE HERMIT.

"Great was her horror when he revealed himself to be none other than Ravana."

From a painting by Ravi Varma.

Sita answered that she was the wife of Rama and could belong to no other lord, whereupon Ravana seized her by force, threw her into his aerial chariot, and flew away with her.

It was a terrible journey over the tops of the trees, and the crests of the mountains. Sita's thought was not for herself but for Rama, and she cast about how she might leave some token to show by what way she had gone. As the chariot sped above a hill, she saw some monkeys playing on the hillside, and she threw down her yellow veil and her golden ornaments, in the hope that they might pick them up.

Over the land went the chariot, and over sea, till it reached Lanka, where Ravana shut up Sita in a palace guarded by female Rakshasas.

3. THE ARMY OF MONKEYS.

When Rama and Lakshman came back to the hut, and found that Sita was gone, they hunted for her, far and wide. At length they heard from the Vulture-Raja, who had seen her in the aerial chariot, that she had been carried off to Lanka.

On their way southwards, they met the Raja of the Monkeys, who had been dethroned by his brother. Rama helped

HANUMAN.

him to regain his throne, and the Monkey-Raja, full of gratitude, promised that his army with its general, Hanuman, should fight for Rama against the Rakshasas.

There is a story that the little grey squirrel was so sorry for Rama when it saw him mourning for Sita, that instead of playing about in the trees, it helped the monkeys to build the bridge between India and Ceylon, great pieces of which are standing in the sea to this day. Rama laid his hand upon the squirrel to bless it, and ever since then you may see the print of his fingers on its back.

Hanuman, who was wisest of all the monkeys, contrived to steal into Lanka, and even to enter the palace where Sita was guarded by the Rakshasas. They were like the creatures seen in bad dreams —some had ears hanging down to their ankles, and some had no ears at all; some had an eye in the middle of their foreheads; some had the heads of dogs, or of swine, or of buffaloes. Every day, Ravana came to ask whether poor Sita would be his wife, and when she refused, he threatened that he would eat her.

While Hanuman was in the palace, he was discovered by some of the guard, and taken before Ravana. Ravana decided not to kill him, but to torture and mock him; he ordered that cotton should be tied to the brave monkey's tail, and set alight.

SITA GUARDED BY THE RAKSHASAS.

From a painting by Ravi Varma.

But Sita heard of the danger of the friend who had come to help her; she prayed to the gods, and the fire did no harm to Hanuman, who escaped out of the clutches of the Rakshasas, and came back to Rama.

After a great deal of fighting between the army of Rama and the Rakshasas, Lanka was taken in a night attack, Ravana killed, and Sita delivered from her prison.

The monkeys all crowded round to see the beautiful lady, and Sita's attendants spoke to them roughly, and would have driven them back. But Rama rebuked his servants, and said that as the monkeys had fought for Sita, they should be allowed to look upon her face, before he took her home to his kingdom.

Some people end this story very sadly, by telling how after he had regained his faithful wife, Rama was so cruel to her that Sita called upon her mother, the Earth, to protect her. The ground opened, and there appeared a beautiful woman who stretched out her hand to Sita, and drew her to sit by her side upon a throne. Then they sank into the depths, and the ground closed over

SITA'S GREAT TRIAL.

"Then they sank into the depths, and the ground closed over their heads."

INTERIOR OF RAMESHWARAM.

This temple was built in memory of Rama's expedition to Ceylon.

their heads. Rama found that he could not live without Sita, and drowned himself.

Other people say that this is not really part of the story, and that Rama and Sita lived happily together.

All over India you find pictures of Rama and Sita, and of Hanuman, and the Hindus tell you "As long as the mountains and rivers continue, so long shall the story of Rama and Sita be told in the world."

SITA, RAMA, LAKSHMAN AND HANUMAN.
IMAGES IN THE TEMPLE OF RAMESHWARAM.

4. THE GOOD EMPEROR ASOKA.

More than two hundred years before the birth of Christ, the Emperor Asoka reigned over nearly the whole of India.

There are many stories about him, some of which may be partly true. One of them says that a Brahman had a daughter, of whom the astrologers foretold that she would have two sons, one, a great monarch, the other a holy man.

When she grew up, she was taken to the palace of an Emperor in a city on the banks of the Ganges, to wait upon his queens. The queens came to know of the prophecy, and were jealous of the Brahman's daughter, fearing that if the Emperor saw her, he would marry her. So they degraded her to doing the work of a barber, thinking that the Emperor would never look at a girl who seemed to be of this caste.

But one day she found an opportunity of speaking to the Emperor, and telling him who she was, and he was so much pleased with her that he made her his wife. She had two sons, one of whom became a holy man, the other was Asoka.

Asoka, as a youth, was rough and unpleasing in his manners. His father cared so little for him that, on hearing that the city of Taxila in the Punjab had revolted, he sent Asoka to subdue it without giving him chariots or any other war equipment.

Many sons would have refused to risk their lives on such an errand, unless they were furnished with all that was needed; Asoka departed at once for Taxila. The legend says that as a reward for his obedience, "the earth opened her bosom," and from it came chariots and all else that he wanted. We need not believe this part of the story, but it is certain that others besides Asoka have succeeded in doing what seemed impossible, by trying their hardest, and not stopping to think about the difficulties in the way.

It turned out that Asoka had no need of war equipment, for the men of Taxila, hearing that he was at their gates, made submission; they had not rebelled against the Emperor, but against unjust ministers who had oppressed them.

After his father's death, Asoka became Emperor. At first, his violent and cruel temper made him feared, until he came under the influence of the teachings of Gautama Buddha, and learned mercy and gentleness.

BUDDHA.

He did not spend his time in wars with other kings; he said that "a conquest by the sword does not deserve the name of conquest," and in his reign of

THE GREAT STUPA AT SANCHI
BUILT IN MEMORY OF BUDDHA.

forty years, there was only one war. He was ready at all times to hear any of his subjects who came to him with petitions. He established hospitals, both for men and for beasts. By the wayside, he planted fruit-trees and dug wells, that men and beasts might be refreshed.

ROCK WITH ASOKA INSCRIPTION.

The law which he taught his subjects, still to be seen engraved upon rocks and pillars in various parts of India, was a law of "mercy and charity, truth and purity." It bade the people hearken to

ASOKA PILLAR.

VIEW OF LOWER PORTION SHOWING INSCRIPTION.

their parents, show mercy to all living things, speak the truth, reverence their teachers, and be courteous to all their relations.

THE "LAT" OR STONE PILLAR OF ASOKA AT DELHI.

When Asoka died, he was remembered as "the Loving-minded One, the Beloved of the Gods."

5. THE PALACE BUILT BY ST. THOMAS.

There were Christians among the people of India long before any Europeans came thither, and there is a story which tells how they learned their faith.

When the twelve Apostles were commanded to go out into the world, and preach the Gospel to every creature, it was the lot of St. Thomas to be sent to India. He knew not how to reach it, and he lamented and complained until St. Peter, the Chief of the Apostles, consented to go with him, and set him upon his way.

Travelling together, they came to a city in which they found a merchant, who had come all the way from India to find a craftsman who should be able to build a palace for Gondophorus, his king.

When St. Thomas heard this, he went to the merchant, saying "If you would buy a slave for your king, take me. I can build temples, palaces, and ships, and I can make ploughs, and just measures and true balances. Moreover, I can heal the sick."

So the merchant bought St. Thomas for three pieces of gold; and St. Thomas gave the gold to the poor, and bade farewell to St. Peter, and went with his master to India.

When they reached the city where Gondophorus dwelt, the King rejoiced to know that here was the architect for his palace. He opened his treasury, and brought forth stores of gold and silver and gems, which he gave to St. Thomas, commanding him to build a palace fairer than any in the land. Then he went away to a distant part of his kingdom, and did not return for two years.

When he came back, he expected to find the palace ready for him. During his absence, St. Thomas had sought out the poor, and given alms to them; he had healed the sick; he had comforted those who were in trouble. The city was full of joy and gladness, where had been misery and suffering. But nothing was left of the King's treasures, and not one stone of the palace had been raised upon another.

Then the King was filled with anger, and he commanded that St. Thomas should be thrown into prison, meaning to put him to a cruel death.

Just at this time, the King's brother was seized with illness, and lay for four days in a trance, as if he were dead. On the fourth day, he opened his eyes, sat upright, and thus spake to the King:—"I have been where the angels showed me a palace of gold and silver and gems, wondrous to behold; and they said, 'This is the palace that Thomas the architect hath built for thy brother, King Gondophorus.'"

Then the King ran with haste to the dungeon, and released the Saint; and St. Thomas said to him, "O King, there are in heaven rich palaces without number, which were prepared from the beginning of the world for those who gain them by faith and by charity. Your riches may prepare the way for you to such a palace, but they cannot follow you thither."

Then the King and all his court were baptized.

After this, the Saint journeyed about India, teaching and preaching, till he suffered martyrdom, being pierced with a lance as he knelt at the foot of a cross that he had made, at the place afterwards called "St. Thomas's Mount," in Madras.

How much of this story is true, we do not know. From very early days, the

Christian church has had a tradition that St. Thomas preached in India, where he baptized the three Wise Men who brought gifts to Bethlehem. When the Portuguese came to India, many hundred years

ST. THOMAS'S MOUNT, MADRAS.

later, they believed that they found the body of the Saint. It is certain that there have been Christians in Southern India, long before Christianity was known in other parts of the country.

PART II.

THE MUSLIM INVASION.

STORIES OF MAHMUD THE IDOL-BREAKER.

6. THE MERCIFUL SLAVE.
7. THE SULTAN AND THE IDOL.

(SOMNATH WAS TAKEN 1026.)

STORIES OF THE LAST HINDU KING OF DELHI.

8. THE WEDDING OF RAI PITHORA.
9. THE BATTLE ON THE PLAIN.

(DELHI WAS TAKEN 1206.)

A HINDU TEMPLE.

6. THE MERCIFUL SLAVE.

If you travelled among the Afghan mountains, to the North-West of India, until you came to the town of Ghazni, you would see at some little distance from the town, two lofty minarets and a tomb. They are all that is left of the old capital of the mountain kingdom of Ghazni, where, nine hundred years ago, you would have found a university, a library, a mosque full of gold and silver ornaments, and other splendid buildings—all founded by the Sultan who sleeps in that tomb, Mahmud "the Idol-breaker."

Mahmud's father, like many rulers in the East of his time, had been a slave. It is said that one day, when hunting, he caught a tiny fawn. He was riding away with it, when he saw its mother following him, uttering such piteous cries, that he was sorry for her, and set the fawn down upon the ground. It scampered away to its mother, and as they went, the mother turned back, two or three times, and looked at the slave, as if she were trying to thank him.

That night, the slave dreamed that the Prophet Mohammad stood beside his bed, and told him that as he had shown mercy to one of God's creatures, in reward God would give him a kingdom.

Some time afterwards, the slave's master, who was Sultan of Ghazni, died, and the slave became Sultan in his stead.

The slave's son, Mahmud, was only a boy when he caught smallpox; he did not die of it, as many did in those days, but his face was so terribly disfigured that he thought that no one would ever love him. So he made up his mind that, since he could not be loved, he would be feared. As soon as he succeeded to his father's throne, he led his army southwards, to invade India.

This was in the year 1000, when the Danes were making forays upon England, where Ethelred the Unready was reigning. While men from the North were invading England, plundering towns, carrying away cattle, slaying women and children, or taking them captive, men from the North were invading India, sacking cities, killing Indian princes and their armies, or selling them for slaves in the markets of Persia. The Danes plundered and destroyed Christian churches, because they were heathen; the Afghans plundered and destroyed Hindu temples,

THREE-HEADED IDOL REPRESENTING BRAHMA, VISHNU AND SIVA.
ELEPHANTA CAVES.

because they were Muslims, and it was part of their religion to break idols. As India, with its wheat, its spices, its sugar-cane, its ivory, gold, silver, and precious stones, was far richer than England, Mahmud and his Afghans profited more by their forays than the Danes.

India was then split up into a number of kingdoms, some large, some small, many of which were at war with each other. If they had united, they might have been able to keep Mahmud off; as it was, he overcame them, one by one. Every year, for six and twenty years, he led an army into India and brought it back to Ghazni, laden with booty.

THE TEMPLE OF SOMNATH.

7. THE SULTAN AND THE IDOL.

The holiest and richest temple in all India was the temple of Siva at Somnath on the shores of Gujarat. The way thither led across a sandy desert, where was little food or water for Mahmud's army. When, after many days of heat and thirst, they stood before the temple, they found its gates closed, and its walls crowded with armed warriors.

For three days, the Hindus and the Afghans fought, and the Hindus had so much the better of it that on the third day the Afghans turned to flee. Mahmud threw himself from his horse, and called upon God and the Prophet, then led his men in a last charge, which broke the enemy's line. Many of the garrison of Somnath were killed, and the rest escaped by sea.

The Afghans pressed into the temple; the pillars were covered with precious stones; the hangings were embroidered with gems; the bell which the worshippers sounded when they came to pray, hung from a huge golden chain. Mahmud thrust his way through the priests of Siva, who were calling in vain upon their god, and stood before the idol.

"Hew it in pieces!" he commanded his followers.

INTERIOR OF THE TEMPLE OF SOMNATH.

Then the priests fell down at his feet, promising to show him where they had hidden the richest treasures of the temple, if he would spare the image.

STONE BULL, SACRED TO SIVA.

TANJORE TEMPLE.

Then Mahmud cried aloud:—

"On the Day of Resurrection, let me hear the call, '*Where is that Mahmud who broke the greatest of the heathen idols?*'—not '*Where is that Mahmud who sold it for gold?*'"

He whirled his mace about his head, and brought it down upon the idol. The image burst asunder, and from inside it poured jewels of far greater value than any in the temple, which the Brahmans had hoped to keep for themselves, if they lost everything else.

After despoiling the temple of everything that it contained, the Afghans began their march back to Ghazni. Some Hindu guides promised to lead them through the deserts; before long, the army found itself wandering among salt pools and ridges of sand, in fearful heat, without a drop of water to drink. Mahmud suspected that the Hindu guides had misled him, and ordered them to be put to the torture.

One of the guides laughed aloud, "We are Brahmans, and priests of Somnath! We have brought you here, where you shall all perish miserably, to avenge our god!"

Some of the Afghans went mad with horror, on hearing these dreadful words. Mahmud fell upon his face in prayer, as he had fallen on the battlefield. Night came on, and still he prayed. Then a meteor blazed in the sky, to the north.

"Lo! a sign from God!" cried Mahmud, and he led his army forthwith in its track. When the sun rose, they had found water, and were saved.

This was Mahmud's last great foray into India.

8. THE WEDDING OF RAI PITHORA.

In the days before the Muslims had conquered India, the bravest in the land was Rai Pithora, Raja of Delhi and Ajmer, whose fort is still standing at Delhi.

He made the great Horse-Sacrifice, which only mighty kings can offer. A horse was consecrated to the gods, and for a year wandered at its will, all men over whose lands it passed owning Rai Pithora for their sovereign lord ("Prithwi Raj"); at the end of the year, the horse was sacrificed, with solemn rites.

Now the Raja of Kanauj was jealous of Rai Pithora, and when he heard of the Horse-Sacrifice, he proclaimed that on a certain day his daughter would choose

RAI PITHORA.

a husband from among the princes of the land. Every one who was to take part in preparing the wedding feast, down to the very scullions who washed the dishes, was to be of royal blood.

From all over India flocked the princes, each hoping to be chosen by the beautiful Princess. Rai Pithora alone did not come, for he had not been invited. The Raja of Kanauj moulded his image in clay, and set it up behind the door, saying that Rai Pithora should act as doorkeeper; this he did in mockery, for the doorkeeper's place at the feast was lowest of all.

Blazing with gold and jewels, the princes waited in the great hall at Kanauj, and the Princess came in, bearing a garland of flowers, which she was to fling to the bridegroom whom she chose. She looked to the right, she looked to the left, and turned quickly round again—and threw the garland round the neck of the clay figure behind the door.

Before her father or her suitors could speak for indignation, an armed man stood in the doorway. The real Rai Pithora had come to the feast, uninvited, and his strong arms seized the Princess, and swung her to the back of his horse that pawed at the gate. Shouting his war-cry, he rode off, fleet as the wind, and though the disappointed princes sprang to horse, and followed him, they could not recover the Princess. For five days Rai Pithora and his followers kept

RAI PITHORA'S TEMPLE, DELHI.

up a running fight with the pursuers, and then they reached the gates of Delhi, and he brought his bride into his palace.

9. THE BATTLE ON THE PLAIN.

For some years Rai Pithora and his Rani lived together in perfect happiness. But their story was not to end happily.

Mahmud the Idol-breaker had left descendants who ruled at Ghazni till they were turned out by another Afghan tribe. Nearly two hundred years after Mahmud's time, the chief of this tribe, Sultan Mohammad Ghori, set to work to invade India, year after year, as Mahmud used to do.

Gradually he made his way towards Delhi, and reached the great plain of Panipat where the throne of Delhi has been lost and won, many times, since the beginning of Indian history. The first time that he came there, Rai Pithora drove him back. A year later, he came with a still greater army. The other rajas were jealous of Rai Pithora, and only the Rana of Chitor came to help him against the invaders.

Rai Pithora asked his wife whether he should fight the Afghans, or try to make terms with them. She answered:—

"To die well is to live for ever. Think not of self, but of immortality."

She armed him for battle, and as he road away, she said to her maidens, "I shall see him again in the mansion of the sun, but never more in Delhi."

She spoke truly, for Rai Pithora's army was cut to pieces by the invading host, and he never came back to her. She put on her bridal dress and jewels, and burned herself upon a funeral pyre. The Afghan chief became the ruler of Delhi, and Muslims have ruled there ever since his time, till the days of Queen Victoria.

PART III.

STORIES OF THE SULTANS OF DELHI.

10. THE STOLEN CHILD.
(ALTAMISH DIED, 1236.)

11. THE BEAUTIFUL PRINCESS.
12. THE CHARMED SWORD.
(ALA-AD-DIN SACKED CHITOR, 1303.)

13. THE SULTAN AND THE HOLY MAN.
(TAGHLAK WAS KILLED, 1325.)

KUTB MINAR.

10. THE STOLEN CHILD.

At the time when Mohammad Ghori was invading India, there was a chief in Turkestan who had many sons. The youngest, Altamish, was cleverer and more lovable than any of his elder brothers, and he was his father's darling.

This made his elder brothers very jealous, and they determined to get him out of the way. One day, they invited him to come with them to see a drove of horses; he went, and his brothers sold him to the horse dealers for a slave.

The horse dealers took him to Bokhara, where was the great slave-market of Central Asia. There he was so lucky as to be bought by a man of high rank, who treated him kindly and gave him a good education.

When Altamish was still quite a little boy, his master sent him to the bazaar to buy grapes. On the way, he lost the money, and began to cry. A faquir came up to him, and asked what was the matter; Altamish told the truth, that he had been sent on an errand, and had lost his master's money. The faquir did not scold him, but taking his hand, led him to the fruit-stalls, bought some grapes, and gave them to him, with these words, "When you attain to dominion and wealth, take care that you show respect to faquirs and pious men, and maintain their rights."

The little slave made the promise, and in after years he kept it, though he never saw his kind friend again.

When he was older, his master sold him to a merchant, who took him to Ghazni, to the Court of Sultan Mohammad. All agreed that a slave so clever, so handsome, and of such noble bearing had never yet been brought to Ghazni, and the Sultan offered to buy him for a thousand gold dinars.

"I can't sell him for that," said the merchant.

"If I cannot buy him for a thousand gold dinars, no one else shall buy him at all," said the Sultan.

After this, no one dared to make any offer for Altamish, and after waiting for a year in the hope of selling him, the merchant was obliged to go back to Bokhara.

He waited there for three years more, and then again brought Altamish to Ghazni; but the Sultan's decree still held, and no one would buy him.

Then there came to Ghazni Aybek, the Sultan's Viceroy in India, who built the wondrous Kutb Mosque at Delhi, and began to build the tallest minaret in

THE KUTB MOSQUE AT DELHI.

the world, the Kutb Minar. He took a fancy to Altamish, and asked the Sultan's leave to buy him.

"I said that no man should buy him in Ghazni, and no man shall," said the Sultan; "if you want him, take him to Delhi, and buy him there."

So Altamish was taken to Delhi, and was soon high in favour of Aybek, who himself had begun life as a slave. In a great battle against the Hindus Altamish fought so bravely that Aybek gave him his freedom, and one of his daughters as a wife.

When Aybek died, Altamish became Sultan of Delhi. He finished building the Kutb Minar, and you may see his tomb near it.

TOMB OF ALTAMISH AT DELHI.

11. THE BEAUTIFUL PRINCESS.

At the time of Mohammad Ghori's invasion, Delhi, Kanauj, and other great Indian kingdoms were ruled by Rajput princes.

A RAJPUT SOLDIER.

The Rajputs are the warrior race of India and none can be braver or more daring than they. But they would not unite against the invaders, and so their kingdoms were overrun by the Muslims.

As the Muslims advanced farther and farther, the Rajputs were driven out of the rich cities and fertile plains, into the deserts and hills of Central India, where their enemies would gain nothing by following them.

Their chief stronghold was Chitor, a city built on a high rock. You may walk among its ruins to-day, and see the empty temples where princes and warriors used to worship, and the stables where they kept the chargers on which they rode to battle; and you may pick wild flowers growing round a palace looking over the lake, which is still called "the Palace of Padmani."

Princess Padmani was wife to one of the bravest of the Rajput princes, who was uncle and guardian to the little Rana of Chitor. All over India, men had heard of her beauty, and at last the fame of it reached the ears of Ala-ad-din, the commander of the army of Delhi.

Ala-ad-din was a cruel, treacherous ruffian, who afterwards murdered the kind old uncle who had brought him up, in order to make himself Sultan of Delhi. He now gathered a host, and marched

PADMANI.

to Chitor, and demanded that Padmani should be given up to him, as he would have the most beautiful woman in India for his wife.

PADMANI-KI-MAHALL.

The Rajputs laughed him to scorn; Chitor, on its rock with massive walls and towers surrounding it, was too strong for his men to capture. Then Ala-ad-din pretended that he had changed his mind, and did not want to carry off the Princess; all he asked was to be allowed to see the reflection of her face in a mirror, and then he would go back to Delhi in peace.

So he came to the palace, and looked in the mirror, and then went away. Padmani's husband escorted him down the hill, as an honoured guest. When

DOOR OF PADMANI-KI-MAHALL.

they came to the outskirts of the Muslim camp, a party of men rose out of ambush and seized the Prince. The treacherous Ala-ad-din sent word to Chitor, "Your Prince shall return to you when you send me the Princess."

Next day, a long procession of palkis came down the hill to Ala-ad-din's camp.

Ala-ad-din was told that Padmani had come with all her ladies, and begged to speak with her husband for the last time. Her palki was set down within a tent, the Prince went in, and came out in a few moments; then he stepped into another palki, and was carried towards Chitor by six bearers.

"Fool!" thought Ala-ad-din, "does he think I really meant to let him go?" And he bade his men stop the palki.

Then the curtains of all the palkis opened, and out sprang, not Padmani and her ladies, but seven hundred armed warriors, who fell upon the Muslims. Padmani had never left the palace. Her husband came back to her in safety. Ala-ad-din, furious at having been tricked and defeated by the Rajputs, struck his camp, and went back to Delhi.

12. THE CHARMED SWORD.

Though Ala-ad-din had been foiled once, he never forgot the face that he had seen in the mirror. When he had made himself Sultan of Delhi, he came back to Chitor with an army, and with battering rams and all sorts of engines, he pelted its walls till it could hold out no longer.

THE GATEWAY OF ALA-AD-DIN
IN THE MOSQUE AT DELHI.

Then the Rajputs opened the gates, and rolled down to the plain, like a river in flood. They knew no fear, but they were few and their foes were many. They were overcome by weight of numbers. When the last had fallen, Ala-ad-din rode into Chitor to find Padmani, but she and all the women had burned themselves on a vast pyre in the vaults below the Rana's palace.

So Ala-ad-din returned to Delhi without the Princess, and there he died miserably. For some time after his death, there was so much fighting and quarrelling among the Muslims that they had no time to harass the Rajputs, who took advantage of this to come back to Chitor, and rebuild it as best they could.

The Rana of Chitor was now Hamir, whose father and eleven brothers had been killed during the siege. When he returned to his city, he found that Ala-ad-din had carried away all its treasures. Hamir cared little for gold or jewels, but he grieved bitterly over the loss of a charmed sword, which had been given long ago to the ancestor of the Ranas of Chitor by the goddess Bhavani.

No one could tell him what had become of it. At last, when he had made supplication at the shrines of all the gods, it was revealed to him that he must look for the sword in the vaults under his palace.

No one had dared to enter those vaults since Padmani and the women of Chitor had died there. It was said that witches and demons flitted about in them, and that a great snake lay coiled in the

THE TOWER OF VICTORY, CHITOR.

This was built by a Rana of Chitor in memory of a great victory over the Muslims.

passage, spitting venom at all who came near. But Hamir had made up his mind to regain the sword, and he went in.

Down, down he went, in pitchy darkness till the passage widened out into a cavern. In the middle of the cavern burned a fire, and round it crouched the witch-wives.

"By what right dost thou break upon our feast?" they cried.

Hamir strode up to the fire, over which hung a great caldron. "I come to claim what is my own," he said, "the sword of my fathers."

Then the witches filled a dish from the caldron, and signed to him to eat. It was horrible to eat with such revellers and horrible was the food set before him, but Hamir did not flinch. When the feast was over, the witches in exchange for his empty plate, gave him the sword.

Back through the darkness to the light of day went Hamir, having rightly earned his heritage by his courage and steadfastness.

13. THE SULTAN AND THE HOLY MAN.

When the cruel Sultan Ala-ad-din died, for many years the people of Delhi were as miserable as during his reign, for the Sultans who came after him were worse even than he. Then at last uprose a great warrior, Taghlak, who had been Ala-ad-din's viceroy in the Punjab, and had driven back the Mongol invaders from the North in nine and twenty battles. The nobles of Delhi elected him as their Sultan, and he chastised evil-doers, and brought peace and order to the land.

Sultan Taghlak built a strong citadel outside Old Delhi, and in it a tomb for himself of red sandstone and white marble. He was in haste to see it finished, because he was an old man, and so he made all the workmen for miles round come to labour upon it. Among them were some men who had been making a tank for a very holy man, Nizam-ad-din Aulia.

The holy man bought oil, and when his workmen came away from the fortress at nightfall, he gave them lamps, and set them to labour at his tank. They durst not refuse and affront the holy man, but they were so weary that they could do no work for the Sultan,

TOMB OF NIZAM-AD-DIN AULIA.

next day. When he found out the reason, Taghlak was very angry, and forbade all men henceforth to give or sell oil to Nizam-ad-din Aulia.

Then the holy man prayed, and a miraculous light rose from the water of the tank when the sun went down, so that the workmen needed no lamps.

Then the Sultan was still more angry and he laid a curse upon the tank, so that the water became noisome, and no one could drink it. (If you go there, you will remember its horrible smell, for the rest of your life.)

FORT OF TAGHLAKABAD AT DELHI

ENCLOSING TOMB OF SULTAN TAGHLAK.

But the holy man cursed the city of Taghlakabad which the Sultan had built, and it has lain desolate ever since his time.

Then the Sultan went into Bengal, and while he was fighting there, his eldest son, Prince Mohammad, plotted with the holy man to seize the throne. This reached the Sultan's ears, and having been victorious in Bengal, he started on his homeward journey, vowing to punish the holy man, whose disciples were very much frightened.

"The Sultan is coming!" they cried.

"It's a far cry to Delhi," said the holy man, calmly telling his beads.

"He will be here to-morrow! let us fly!"

"It's still a far cry to Delhi," said the holy man.

Just outside Delhi, the Sultan was met by Prince Mohammad, who asked him to a feast in a wooden pavilion beside the river. After the feast, there was a parade of elephants, and while Taghlak and his youngest son looked on, the pavilion suddenly collapsed. Mohammad had had it built to fall and kill his father and brother.

The old Sultan's body was found under the ruins, with arms stretched out over his dead boy, as if he had tried to shield him. He was buried in his tomb in the citadel, and Mohammad became Sultan. He had been a cruel son, he proved to be a cruel ruler and every one was glad when his reign ended.

PART IV.

THE GREAT DAYS OF THE MOGHUL EMPIRE.

BABAR.

14. THE ARMY IN THE SNOW.

The next wave of invasion to sweep into India was led by Timur the Tartar, who had conquered Persia, Mesopotamia, and Afghanistan. He came to Delhi, murdering, pillaging, and destroying, stayed there for fifteen days, and went back to Samarkand, leaving ruin and desolation all along his track.

After this, the Sultan of Delhi was of no account, and there was little but revolt and disorder, until another conqueror came from the North, who won Delhi in battle when Henry VIII. was reigning in England.

Babar was the son of the king of a little state beyond the Oxus, now called Khokan; in his time, it was known as Farghana. He was not twelve years old when his father died from an accident, and he had to rule the kingdom, lead the army to battle, and take care of his mother and sister whom he loved very much. His two uncles, like the wicked uncles in a fairy story, tried to take his kingdom away from him, and he had many other enemies.

Sometimes he wore the silken robes of a king, sometimes he wandered over the bleak hillsides, clad in sheepskin with leather brogues upon his feet; but

TIMUR.

wherever he was, in the rose-gardens of a palace, or in a shepherd's smoky hut, he was always a true king—brave, cheerful, courteous, thinking of others besides himself.

When you are older, you can read the book which he wrote, telling his adventures from boyhood nearly to the end of his life. You will read there how he enjoyed a good fight, and how he used to make poetry as he galloped after a flying enemy—how he loved and noticed the beautiful things about him, the flowers, the animals and the stars. There is room here for only one story from this book, which shows how he was ready to take his share of good and bad with his followers.

After many fights and wanderings, Babar made himself King of Kabul, which is nearer to India than Farghana. He had been on a long journey to visit some cousins at Herat, and when he tried to come back over the mountains to Kabul, the snow was falling so heavily that he and his army were nearly lost.

For about a week, they struggled on. Babar and some of the strongest went in front, to trample down the snow, and make it easier for the others. At every step, they sank to the waist or the chest, but still they went on.

"Every one who has spirit does his best at such times," said Babar, "and those who have none are not worth thinking about." After three or four

THE VALLEY OF THE SHADOW OF DEATH, KABUL.

days' hard work, such a fearful snow-storm came on, that they all expected to die. Just then, they came to the mouth of a cave among the rocks, and his officers begged him to take shelter inside it.

But he refused, because the cave was not big enough to hold all his men. "I could not sit there, warm and comfortable," he said, "if my soldiers were cold and wretched in the snowdrifts." So he sat in the snow with them, until a cave was found large enough to hold every one. Babar was none the worse, except for a cold in his ear, and his men must have loved him more than ever.

15. THE CONQUEST OF DELHI.

Babar had been King in Kabul for some years when he marched down to the plains to conquer India. At that time, the Sultan of Delhi was an Afghan, who was detested by every one; his Afghan officials and nobles were hated by the Hindus, because they were foreigners and Muslims, and they quarrelled amongst themselves, so that their big army could not withstand Babar's little army.

The battle was fought on the plain of Panipat, on another part of which the Muslim invaders had overcome Rai Pithora, more than three hundred years ago. The Afghan Sultan was killed,

KABUL.

and his army defeated, and Babar took possession of Delhi and Agra.

In these two cities, he found all manner of treasures, which he shared with his army. His eldest son, Prince Humayun, had protected the family of an Indian raja, who had been killed fighting against Babar, and to show their gratitude, they gave him an enormous diamond. He brought it to his father, who told him to keep it for himself. Some people say it was this very diamond which is now in the Tower of London, having been presented to Queen Victoria.

One of the first things that Babar did was to remember those left behind in Kabul. On a certain day, all the royal ladies, his wives, daughters, sisters, aunts, and others were told to come into the palace garden. When they arrived, they found that it was full of beautiful presents which Babar, in the middle of his fighting, had found time to choose for each one of them—gems, and coins, and gold plates, and the gorgeous Delhi embroideries that look like jewels, and muslins so fine and soft that they could be drawn through a finger-ring. There were so many things that it took three whole days to divide them among the ladies.

BABAR'S GARDEN AT AGRA

WHERE HE PLANTED ROSES AND NARCISSUS.

From a Persian MS. of his Memoirs at the British Museum.

In a little while, Babar had subdued the upper part of India, and could send for the ladies to come to him. Even his aunts came; Babar was especially kind to them, telling his state architect that he must do whatever work they wanted for their palace, before doing anything else. He used to go and see them, every Friday. One day, it was very hot, and his wife said, "The wind is very hot indeed; how would it be if you did not go, this Friday?" But Babar said, "They have no father or brothers; if I do not go to cheer them, who will do it?"—and he went, just as usual.

He felt the heat very much, and often longed for the snowy hills that he was never to see again. He planted roses and narcissus, in remembrance of the gardens where he used to sit and talk with his friends. In the furnace of the Indian plains, he suffered from fever, and grew weaker, month by month. Little more than four years after the battle which made him Emperor of Delhi, he fell very ill and died, while his family, his soldiers, and his nobles all wailed and lamented.

16. THE RANI'S BRACELET.

You will remember how Chitor was taken by Sultan Ala-ad-din. That is known in history as the first sack of Chitor. The second sack came in the days when Humayun, Babar's son, was Emperor of Delhi.

Nothing could teach the Rajput princes not to quarrel amongst themselves, and their disputes made it easy for the Muslim ruler of Gujarat, Bahadur Shah, to invade Rajputana and besiege Chitor.

Then, when the foe was at the gates, nearly all the Rajput princes forgot their feuds, and gathered to defend the city. All fought bravely, women as well as men. The Rana of Chitor, Bikramajit, was not there, but his mother, the old Rani, who had caused many of the quarrels, in days gone by, put on armour, took up shield and spear, and led a sally against the besiegers. She died like a warrior, but she could not drive back the men of Gujarat. Bahadur Shah had brought very heavy cannon, and had European gunners and engineers. The walls of Chitor began to crack, and the garrison saw that they could not hold out much longer.

HUMAYUN.

The next heir to Bikramajit was his little half-brother, Udai Singh, whose mother thought of a way to save her son. There is a very old custom among the Rajputs that a woman may send a bracelet to any man whom she pleases, and claim his help at need. As soon as he puts the bracelet on, he becomes her brother, and is bound to do whatever she may ask.

The Rani wove a bracelet of floss-silk and spangles, and called a trusty messenger. "Make your way through the enemy's lines," she said, "ride hard till you find the Emperor Humayun, and give him this bracelet from me."

The messenger rode long and rode far; the Emperor Humayun was not in his palace at Delhi, or his rose-gardens at Agra. It was many weary days and nights ere he found him in Bengal, and laid the bracelet at his feet.

To his joy, the Emperor took it up, and bound it about his wrist. "What would the Rani have of me?" he asked; "she shall have her desire, were it my strongest fortress."

"For herself the Rani asks nothing," answered the messenger, "but she implores her brother to save her son from his enemies."

Then Humayun led his army into Rajputana. But instead of hastening to attack Bahadur Shah, he sent letters bidding him raise the siege, to which Bahadur Shah paid no heed.

The city walls were falling down under the Gujarat cannon; the garrison prepared to make a good end. Little Udai Singh was smuggled through the enemy's lines, in charge of a trusty henchman. His mother and the other women mounted the funeral pyre, and the men rushed down through the gates, to die sword in hand.

A fortnight afterwards, Humayun arrived, too late to save the garrison and the brave Rani, but in time to chase away Bahadur Shah, whose army melted away in all directions, leaving the spoil of Chitor behind them. Humayun sent for Bikramajit to rule in Chitor, and Udai Singh was brought back to the palace.

17. THE FAITHFUL NURSE.

Rana Bikramajit was neither wise nor courteous in his dealings with his nobles. Soon after he came back to Chitor, he had offended them so grievously that they deposed him, and appointed a cousin, Bunbeer, as Regent for Udai Singh, who was only six years old.

Udai Singh's nurse whose name was Punna ("the diamond"), had a boy of the same age as the little Prince, who was brought up with him. One evening, after playing together, as usual, they had their supper of rice and milk, and then fell asleep, lying on the same couch, while the nurse watched over them. Suddenly, from the rooms where the women lived, there rose screams and cries. Punna heard, and knew that it was the wailing for the dead.

In hurried one of the palace barbers. "They are wailing for Bikramajit," he said. "You know how the nobles deposed him, and made Bunbeer Regent; Bunbeer has killed him, to make himself Rana."

"Then he will kill my Prince too," said the nurse, "for while he lives, Bunbeer cannot be Rana. Help me to save him!"

She caught up the little Prince, tore off his silk coat and jewels, and put him in a great basket in which fruit had been brought, piling leaves on the top, so as to hide him.

"Take him, and hide in the dry riverbed, beyond the city walls," she said; "wait there till I come." The barber took the basket, and walked out of the palace. None of the guards stopped him. They were used to see him carrying scraps from the kitchen home to his family, and they never thought of looking into the basket.

Meanwhile, Punna dressed her own little boy in the Prince's clothes and jewels. She had scarcely finished when the hangings of the doorway were torn to one side, and there stood Bunbeer, sword in hand.

"Woman, show me the Prince!" he cried. The poor nurse could not make herself speak; she raised her hand and pointed to the couch where her son lay, and Bunbeer killed him.

As soon as she could get out of the palace, Punna slipped down to the river-bed, where she found the barber, and Udai Singh, who luckily had not woke or cried since he was put into the basket. They made their way across the country by lonely tracks, trying to find some prince or chief who would shelter the little Rana; but none who dwelt near Chitor would face the risk of Bunbeer's discovering him.

So the nurse had to go farther still, into the eastern hill, through ravines, along precipices, over torrents, among wild beasts and wild men, till she came to the fortress of Komulmir where lived a Jain chief. He listened to her story, and promised to protect Udai Singh; but the nurse must leave him, since he must pass for the chief's nephew, and a Jain boy could not have a Rajput nurse.

THE FORTRESS OF KOMULMIR.

So she went back to her home, and waited alone for seven long years. At the end of that time, Bunbeer had made himself detested by the nobles of Chitor.

THE RUINS OF CHITOR.

When they heard from the nurse that Udai Singh was still alive, they made him Rana, and drove out Bunbeer. Sad to say, he proved one of the worst Ranas ever known, and it was in his reign that Chitor was taken by the Emperor Akbar.

This was the third sack, and ever since then, the city has lain in ruins.

18. THE CRUEL UNCLE.

Babar's son, Humayun, was not such a man as his father, and in many ways he had harder work to do. The Moghuls were foreigners in India; they belonged to a race differing more from the Hindus than the Hindus from the English. They had won Delhi because they were the stronger, and they could keep it only so long as they remained the stronger.

Some of the army that had conquered with Babar were dead, and some had gone back to their homes in the North. Humayun had enemies all round him, and worse than any of them were his three brothers, who were jealous of him, and rebelled continually against him.

He was turned out of Delhi, and for a long time wandered up and down, like his father, a king without a kingdom. At last, he got possession of his father's city of Kabul, and settled there, with his wife and his little son, Akbar. Even then, he had no peace, for one of his brothers, Prince Kamran, gathered an army, and tried to get the kingdom for himself. Humayun went in pursuit of him, and had not gone far when he was taken ill. For many days, he lay in a trance, knowing nothing of what was going on, kept alive by the juice of pomegranates, which his wife squeezed into his mouth.

When he came to himself, there was very bad news for him. While he lay ill, Kamran had seized upon the fort of Kabul, and upon little Akbar who had been left in it.

The poor father marched back to Kabul, through the heavy snow, and stood at the gates of the fort, with his officers round him, to summon his brother to surrender.

They saw ropes hanging from the battlements, and tied to those ropes were three poor little boys, the sons of two of the nobles at Humayun's side; these boys were Akbar's play-fellows, and had been left in Kabul with him. "I have killed three other boys," said Kamran, "and I will kill these, and throw their bodies over the wall, unless their fathers will desert my brother, and fight for me."

THE FORT OF KABUL.

One of the fathers, who was Humayun's prime minister, calmly answered, as he watched his sons dangling in the air,

"The children must die some day, and how can they die better than now, to serve their Emperor?"

Some say that Kamran was ashamed at this noble answer, and that he did no further harm to the children. Others

TOMB OF HUMAYUN AT DELHI.

say that when Humayun's guns opened fire upon the fort, Kamran set his little nephew, Akbar, on the battlements, hoping either that the Emperor's gunners would cease firing, for fear of hurting the baby, or that a shot would kill him. Then out rushed Akbar's nurse, and stooped over him, covering him with outstretched arms, so that no shot could touch him unless it first went through her body.

In spite of all he did, Kamran was obliged to surrender the fort. He ended his days miserably, blind, and a prisoner, while Humayun went back to India, and regained Delhi.

Six months after his return, Humayun fell down a staircase, and died. Akbar, who was then a boy of thirteen, became Emperor.

19. THE WOUNDED ENEMY.

Akbar had to fight for his throne.

The Afghans had invaded India, and a Hindu named Himu had defeated the Moghul army at Delhi, and proclaimed himself Raja. Nearly all Akbar's councillors advised the young Emperor to retreat to Kabul as fast as he could, thinking that he had no chance of ruling in India.

There were two persons who did not mean to run away; one was Akbar himself, and the other was Bairam Khan, an old officer who had fought many times by

AKBAR.

Humayun's side, and had been appointed Regent until Akbar should be old enough to govern for himself. They prevailed, and the Moghul army and the army of Himu met for battle on the great plain of Panipat, where Akbar's grandfather, Babar, had won the throne of Delhi, thirty years before.

Himu was one of the most extraordinary men in History. Many great generals have risen from being common soldiers, and some have been feeble in body; General Wolfe, when he took Quebec, was dying of consumption; one of the most celebrated French generals was a hunchback. Himu rose, not from the ranks, but from a chandler's shop, to the command of troops, and though he won two and twenty battles, he was so weak and sickly that he could never sit a horse.

He came now to his last battle, in a howdah on the back of his favourite elephant, and led a charge which broke the Moghul line. But the Moghuls, who had been warned by Bairam that it would be waste of time to run away, as their homes in Kabul were a thousand miles distant, kept up such a persistent fire of arrows and javelins that the elephants could not face it, and turned round, and charged into their own ranks.

Just at this moment, a Moghul arrow pierced Himu's eye; he fell on the floor of the howdah, and his army, thrown into confusion by the stampeding elephants, and thinking he was killed, broke and fled in all directions. Some of the Moghul cavalry surrounded Himu's elephant, and drove it to the Moghul camp, where Akbar was kept by Bairam's orders.

Bairam was delighted when he saw Himu lying half-dead. He had not allowed the Emperor to risk his life in the battle; nevertheless, here was an opportunity for the boy to earn the title of "Ghazi." (A Ghazi is a Muslim who has slain an "infidel," that is to say, one who is not of his religion.)

"Prove your sword upon this infidel!" he cried.

Akbar turned fiercely upon his guardian. "How can I strike a man who is as good as dead? It is on strength and sense that a king's sword is proved."

Bairam's answer was to draw his own sword, and strike off Himu's head with one blow, while Akbar burst into tears of shame and indignation.

Akbar never forgot or forgave that blow; as soon as he could, he took the government out of Bairam's hands, and when sixteen years old, he was Emperor in deed as well as in name.

AKBAR'S TOMB AT SECUNDRA, NEAR AGRA.

20. THE COMING OF THE ENGLISH.

In the reign of Queen Elizabeth three Englishmen journeyed to India, with a letter from their Queen to the Emperor. It was nearly thirty years since Himu's defeat, and Akbar had grown from a boy into the greatest and noblest ruler that India has ever known.

FATEHPUR SIKRI

BUILT BY EMPEROR AKBAR.

He was keeping his Court in Fatehpur Sikri, a city which he had built near Agra. No Emperor has lived there, since his time. As you wander about it, you may see much that the Englishmen saw, more than three hundred years ago.

PANCH MAHALL, FATEHPUR SIKRI.

There is the Emperor's bedroom, which he called the "House of Dreams," where he used to sit, night after night, talking with his friends. There is the courtyard, marked out in squares like a chess-board, where he used to play chess with living pieces; the winner of the game carried off the pawns, who were sixteen

AKBAR LISTENING TO ARGUMENTS UPON RELIGION.

beautiful slave-girls. There are the palaces built for his chief wives, who were of different religions. One was a Hindu princess, and had a little temple for her gods; another was a Portuguese lady, and Akbar sent for a Portuguese artist to paint a picture of Our Lady and the Angel Gabriel over her door. (You can still see the Angel's golden wings, if you look carefully.)

There is the big hall, where once a week the Emperor used to sit, listening to arguments upon religion between Muslims, Hindus, Jesuit missionaries from Goa, and others.

But the courtyards are empty, and the halls are bare. When the Englishmen came to the city, they saw the courtyards spread with silk and soft carpets. They saw the Emperor's cavalry ride by, dressed in cloth of gold, and they saw hundreds of elephants, some of them decked with gold and rubies, going past the throne, and giving the salute. They saw the nobles stand round the throne, covered with jewels, and below the throne stood a man, black-haired and black-eyed, with sturdy body and very long arms, dressed in plain white muslin. This was the Emperor Akbar.

INTERIOR OF DIWAN-I-KHAS,

FATEHPUR SIKRI.

P. S. B. L H.

He read the letter in which Queen Elizabeth asked him to give the three Englishmen leave to travel through his kingdom. One of the three was a jeweller, and he stayed for some time at the Court, working for Akbar. The second went on northwards to the Punjab, and no one knows what became of him. The third, whose name was Ralph Fitch, went back to England, and founded the first Company of London Merchants trading with India.

About a hundred years later, this Company joined with another, and was known from that time as "The East India Company." This, from a body of merchants, gradually became the greatest power in India. After the Indian Mutiny, in 1858 the Company came to an end, and the territories it had held in India were brought under the direct rule of the British Government.

21. A NOBLE QUEEN.

To the south of Hindustan is the tableland of the Deccan, which like Hindustan for many years, had been ruled by

Muslims. In the time of Akbar, there were five kingdoms in the Deccan; two of these were Ahmadnagar and Bijapur.

BULAND DARWAZA, FATEHPUR SIKRI,

ERECTED BY AKBAR TO COMMEMORATE HIS VICTORIOUS CAMPAIGN IN THE DECCAN.

Towards the end of Akbar's reign, the Sultan of Ahmadnagar died; he left no son, and no less than four princes claimed his throne. One of these, his nephew, was a mere child, and seemed to have little chance against the others. His guardian was Chand Bibi ("the Resplendent Lady"), one of the noblest women in Indian history.

The people of Ahmadnagar were devoted to her, and when she appealed to them, they agreed to support the boy-Sultan. But one of the other claimants

CHAND BIBI.

to the throne made appeal to Akbar, who sent an army to back him up, and another called for help to the Sultan of Bijapur. Altogether, there were four armies marching down upon Ahmadnagar.

Chand Bibi did not lose heart; she wrote to the Sultan of Bijapur, who was her kinsman. "If we fight one against the other, the Emperor of Delhi will destroy us, one by one; rather let us unite against Delhi."

Her wise words touched the Sultan's heart, and he became her ally. Meanwhile, she defended Ahmadnagar against the Moghul army. By day and night she was on the walls, with the Moghul shot raining around her, or in the darkness under the earth, where the mines were laid.

Once, the enemy fired a mine, and made a great breach in the walls; the defenders were so much startled that they fled from their posts, leaving the way open to the storming party. Then they saw coming down to them a slight figure in richly decorated armour, with a silver veil floating over the helmet; it was the Queen. She called upon her men, she led them back to the wall. All day long they stood in the breach, keeping off the Moghuls, and the silver veil gleamed wherever the danger was sorest; then, when night came, and the Moghuls drew off, she toiled with the garrison, who brought wood, stones, and earth, and built up the wall again. The people of Ahmadnagar have a story that, when ammunition ran short, the Queen made balls of copper, then of silver, then of gold, and at last, when nothing else was left, fired away her jewels.

Then the Moghuls heard that the army of Bijapur was coming to drive them away, so they broke up their camp, and made peace with the Queen.

Unluckily, this is not the end of the story. After all that she had done for them, the people of Ahmadnagar turned against Chand Bibi. Her own prime minister betrayed her to Delhi, and before the year was out, another Moghul army was on the way to Ahmadnagar, where some of the troops had revolted, and were besieging the Queen. She was obliged to make terms with Delhi. While she strove to gain the utmost for her nephew and her people, some of the rebels told her soldiers that the Queen was betraying them to the Moghuls. The soldiers in fury broke into the women's rooms, calling for her; she faced them, and fell beneath their swords.

THE WALLS AND MOAT OF BIJAPUR.

A few days later, the Moghul army stormed Ahmadnagar, and slaughtered every man in the garrison. But though they might avenge her, nothing could bring back the noble Queen.

22. THE STORY OF A BABY.

In the days when Queen Elizabeth ruled in England, a Persian nobleman who had fallen into poverty, was journeying to India with his wife and family, to seek his fortune at the Court of Akbar.

They had reached Kandahar when a baby was born to them. They had three other children, and no money to feed them, and this was only a girl. So they laid her down by the roadside, and left her there.

A rich merchant who was travelling by the same caravan as the Persians, when he passed along the road saw the poor forsaken little baby, and picked her up. "I will bring up this child as my own," he said. "Is there any woman in the caravan who will take care of her on the journey?"

The baby's mother came forward, and took the baby. Before long, she confessed to the merchant that it was her own child.

When they reached India, the merchant befriended the Persian and his eldest son, and recommended them to the Emperor, who gave them employment. When she grew older, Muhr-i-Nisa ("Seal of Womankind") as they had called the little girl, used to go with her mother to visit the ladies of the Court.

One day, she had slipped away from every one, and was sitting all alone in a corner of the Palace garden, when a boy carrying two doves caught sight of her. It was the Emperor's eldest son.

"Hold these for me till I come back," he said, thrust the doves into her hands, and hurried away.

Muhr-i-Nisa was dreaming of all manner of beautiful things, and forgot the doves. Suddenly, she looked down, and saw that one of them had escaped—and just at that minute, the Prince came back.

"Where is the other dove?" he cried.

"My lord, I let it go."

"Stupid!" stormed the Prince, "how did you do that?"

"So, my lord!" she answered, throwing out her arms, and letting the other dove fly away.

The Prince fell in love with her, there and then, and would have married her

JAHANGIR.

when he was a little older, but the Emperor would not hear of it. Muhr-i-Nisa was given as a wife to a young Afghan in the Emperor's service, who took her to Bengal, where he had a governorship.

After Akbar's death, the Prince became the Emperor Jahangir. Hearing complaints about this governor, he sent for him to answer them. The Afghan struggled with the men who came to arrest

NUR JAHAN.

him, and was killed. Muhr-i-Nisa was sent to Court as a prisoner.

Jahangir would not see her, and for four years she lived quietly among the other women.

Every year a great fair was held in the Palace, and the ladies of the Court sold at the stalls. At one of these fairs Jahangir noticed some paintings and embroideries, so beautiful that he was sure they could be the work of none but Muhr-i-Nisa. But where was Muhr-i-Nisa? She was not selling, with the other ladies. She was sitting in her room, at work with her slaves, when suddenly Jahangir entered.

No sooner had he looked upon her than he loved her more passionately than ever. In a little while, he made her his Empress, and changed her name, first, to Nur-Mahal ("Light of the Palace"), then to Nur-Jahan ("Light of the World").

His marriage was the best day's work that Jahangir ever did for himself. Nur-Jahan was wise as she was devoted; when he was actually made prisoner by a rebellious general, it was she who contrived to free him, when his army had failed to do it.

After his death she lived for many years, devoting herself to good works, and daily praying beside his tomb at Lahore.

TOMB OF JAHANGIR AT LAHORE.

23. THE STORY OF THE TAJ MAHAL.

Nearly every one has heard of the Taj Mahal at Agra. It is one of the wonders of the world.

It was built by Shah Jahan, son of the Emperor Jahangir. Nur Mahal had no children after her marriage to Jahangir, but she had a niece married to Shah

THE TAJ MAHAL AT AGRA.

Jahan. In history, this niece is called by various names; the easiest to remember is Mumtaz-i-Mahal, which means "The Chosen of the Palace." We hear

SHAH JAHAN.

very little about her, but she must have been a good and loving wife, for Shah Jahan was devoted to her while she lived, and would never marry again, after her death.

When Jahangir died, Shah Jahan succeeded him as Emperor; only a year later, Mumtaz-i-Mahal died. The Emperor was heart-broken, and found his only comfort in the children she had left to him.

THE DIWAN-I-AMM (HALL OF PUBLIC AUDIENCE) IN THE PALACE AT AGRA.

On the banks of the Jumna, at Agra, he built a palace which must have been like an enchanted palace in a fairy tale. There was an Audience Hall, where he used to give justice, robed in cloth of gold, with a spray of diamonds in his turban and strings of huge pearls round his neck. He sat upon the "Peacock Throne"—a throne of gold covered with gems, over which two jewelled peacocks spread their tails, and the Koh-i-Nur hung down from the canopy. In the pavilion, he sat with the royal ladies, and fished in the tank below. In a

THE SCALES OF JUSTICE

ON THE CARVED MARBLE SCREEN THROUGH WHICH PETITIONS WERE RECEIVED.

beautiful hall looking out upon a garden, the queens and princesses received the ladies who came to visit them. Their bathrooms had walls of looking-glass, and ceilings that glittered like silver, and rows of lamps flashed upon the water as it fell into a marble fountain. There was the "Pearl Mosque" where they prayed, and most beautiful of all, the Jasmine Tower overlooking the river, which was ornamented with flowers made of precious stones.

THE PEARL MOSQUE (MOTI MASJID), AGRA.

But Mumtaz-i-Mahal could have no share in all this splendour, for she was dead. Therefore, Shah Jahan determined that she should have the most beautiful tomb ever made for any woman.

On the opposite bank of the river, he made a garden, and within the garden he built a tomb of white marble, and sent for craftsmen from Italy to inlay

TOMBS OF
MUMTAZ-I-MAHAL AND SHAH JAHAN
IN THE TAJ MAHAL.

SARCOPHAGI
IN INTERIOR OF THE TAJ MAHAL.

it with coloured stones. Beneath the dome in the centre, he laid the body of Mumtaz-i-Mahal.

When Shah Jahan grew old, his third son, Aurangzib, determined to get the throne for himself. He put two of his brothers to death, he drove another out

THE JASMINE TOWER.

of the country, and he kept Shah Jahan a prisoner for the rest of his life. The poor old Emperor was shut up in the Pearl Mosque, with his eldest daughter, the Princess Jahanara, who chose to be a captive with her father, rather than live at her brother's Court.

THE TAJ MAHAL
FROM THE JASMINE TOWER.

When he was dying, Shah Jahan begged that he might be allowed to look once more on the Taj Mahal. He was carried to the Jasmine Tower, and lay there, gazing across the river, till he died. Aurangzib had refused to let him go to the Taj Mahal while he lived, but his dead body was taken thither, and buried beside his wife.

THE FORT, AGRA.

PART V.

THE DECLINE OF THE MOGHUL EMPIRE.

STORIES OF SIVAJI.

24. SIVAJI AND THE ENGLISH.
25. THE ESCAPE FROM AGRA.

(SIVAJI DIED, 1680.)

26. TWO ENGLISH DOCTORS.

27. THE COMING OF NADIR SHAH.
28. THE SACK OF DELHI.

(NADIR SHAH CAME TO DELHI, 1738.)

STORIES OF THE SIKHS.

29. GURU NANAK AND GURU ARJUN.
30. GURU TEG BAHADUR AND GURU GOBIND.

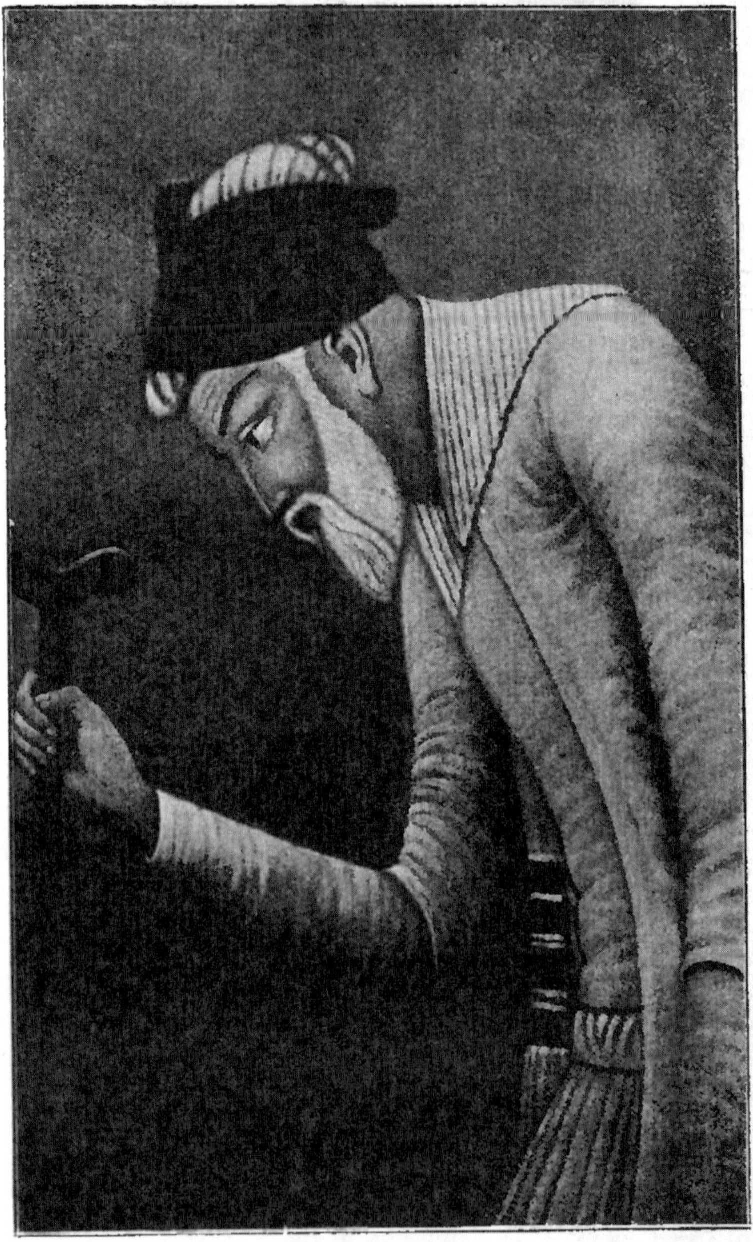

AURANGZIB.

24. SIVAJI AND THE ENGLISH.

Having deposed his father and killed his brothers, Aurangzib meant to be a great and good Emperor. But after such a beginning, nothing could go well with him, and he was to know little but trouble and sorrow throughout his long reign of fifty years.

The cause of some of his worst troubles was Sivaji the Maratha.

Sivaji was brought up by a mother who was as beautiful as she was clever. She told him the old Hindu legends, and taught him to dream of the time when he would be a man, and should drive the Muslims before him as Rama drove the Rakshasas. He never learned to write so much as his own name, but ere his beard was grown, he could lead a foray, and he knew every inch of the wild glens of the Konkan, where the Marathas lived.

His feudal lord was the Sultan of Bijapur; for many years Sivaji defied him, harrying his territory and plundering his towns. The Sultan sent an expedition under Afzul Khan, one of his most trusted officers, to bring him to order. Sivaji came to meet Afzul, pretending that he would submit. As the Khan embraced him in friendship, Sivaji

SIVAJI.

struck at him with the "tiger's claws"— crooked steel blades which he had hidden in his closed hand—and then cut off his head with his sword. It was a cruel treacherous deed, but Sivaji believed that he was acting by command of the goddess Bhavani, who had chosen him to overthrow the Muslims.

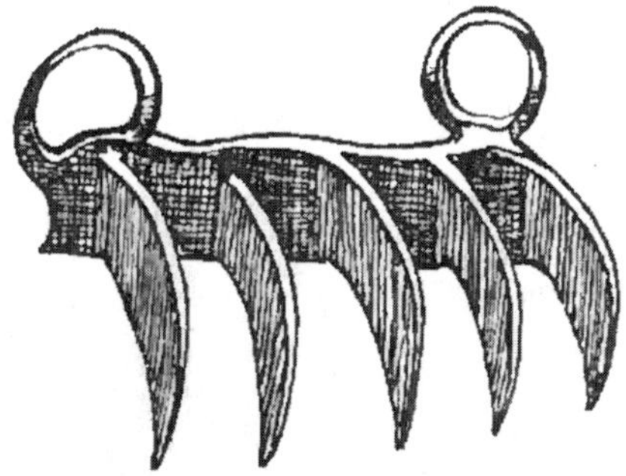

"TIGER'S CLAWS."

After this, the Marathas over-ran the country, and plundered not only the towns belonging to the Sultan of Bijapur, but also some of those belonging to the Emperor of Delhi. One of the places they attacked was Surat, where the English merchants had what was called a factory—that is to say, a trading centre. Luckily, Sir George Oxinden who was at the head of the factory was one of those men who made the name of Englishmen respected in the East. When Sivaji entered Surat, Sir George held the factory against him, with a handful of men. Sivaji threatened to raze the factory to the ground, and not to spare a life; Oxinden sent back word, "We are here to defend this place to the last man, so do not delay your coming upon us." Then the English made a sally, and routed Sivaji's guards.

SURAT FORT.

After this, a Moghul army came up, and Sivaji retreated, having burned part of the city, carrying away rich plunder of gold and silver, pearls and precious stones. A number of the people of Surat had taken refuge in the factory, and clamoured that some reward might be given to Oxinden, who had saved them from the Marathas. The commander of the Moghul army offered him a robe of honour, a horse, and a sword. "These are for a soldier," said Oxinden, "but we are merchants, and what we ask is favour in our trade."

He would have nothing for himself, and thought only of the advancement of his country. He gained what he asked; from that time, the English were relieved from some of the customs duties which had to be paid by other nations trading in the Emperor's dominions.

25. THE ESCAPE FROM AGRA.

Not content with his raids on land, Sivaji built a fleet, and turned pirate on the high seas. When he took to stopping the ships bringing Muslim pilgrims from Mecca, the Emperor Aurangzib could endure it no longer, and sent an army to deal with him. Sivaji surrendered, and promised to give up some of the forts that he had taken, and to serve in the imperial army.

He was ordered to Agra, to do homage to the Emperor. Aurangzib could not believe that this common-looking little man could be a dangerous enemy, and treated him so contemptuously, speaking of him as "the mountain rat," that Sivaji was affronted, and asked leave to go home. When he had no answer to this, and found that his house was watched by a guard who followed him wherever he went, he saw that he was in great danger.

So he took to his bed, where he lay groaning and sighing, declaring that he was very ill. Daily he sent offerings to Brahmans and other holy men, entreating them to pray for his recovery, and among these offerings were always large covered baskets full of sweetmeats.

One day, a spy came into Agra, with the news that Sivaji was at large. The kotwal hurried to Sivaji's house, where the guards were still watching. They swore that he had never left it. To make sure, they looked inside, and reported that he was lying asleep, on his couch. His face was covered with a muslin scarf, but they could see his hand on which was a gold ring that he always wore.

The kotwal had just gone home, when in came another spy, who was sure that Sivaji was a hundred miles away. Back hurried the kotwal, and went into the

GOL GUMBAZ,

TOMB OF MOHAMMAD ADIL SHAH, KING OF BIJAPUR,

room where the sleeping man lay, and tore off the scarf. The face underneath was not that of Sivaji, but of one of his followers who had put on his clothes and his ring to deceive the guards.

Sivaji and his son had been carried out of the house in two of the big baskets, into which the guard had never troubled to look, thinking they contained sweetmeats. At a place outside Agra, swift horses were waiting, and Sivaji took his son before him, and rode hard to Mathura.

There he and some fifty of his men shaved off their beards and whiskers, smeared themselves with ashes, and pretended to be Hindu faquirs. In this disguise they had travelled some part of their way home, when they came to a place where the alarm had been given that Sivaji had escaped.

Seeing a party of faquirs enter the town, the governor threw them all into prison, till he could find out who they were. On the second night he was told that one of them wished to speak to him alone. "I am Sivaji," said the faquir. "In these hollow sticks I have gold mohurs, and a ruby and a pearl of great price. If you send our heads to Agra, you will not be able to keep the jewels; if you let us go, the Emperor will know nothing about it."

THE RAUZA OF IBRAHIM, BIJAPUR.

The governor took the bribe, and released the faquirs next day. Sivaji came safely home, and for fourteen years until his death continued to raid the territory of Delhi and Bijapur, to sack towns, and to levy tribute, without the Emperor or the Sultan being able to suppress him.

26. TWO ENGLISH DOCTORS.

There have been many builders of the British Empire. Some of the best of them have been the English doctors in foreign lands, who have tried to cure the sickness and suffering that they saw round them, without thinking of themselves. Our empire in India owes much to two doctors.

When first the London merchants began to trade with India, after the three Englishmen had visited Akbar's Court, they were allowed one small trading-station, or "factory," as it was called, at Surat on the western coast; but their trade was carried on with great difficulty. The Portuguese and the Dutch, who had been trading in India for some time, were very jealous of the new Company, and did all that they could to spite it, and to get it into trouble with the Customs officers of the Emperor of Delhi. The Company was above all desirous of leave to trade in Bengal, but this was refused to them.

The Princess Jahanara, daughter of the Emperor Shah Jahan, had a favourite dancing-girl. Somehow or other, this girl's skirt caught fire, one day,

THE DUTCH TOMBS, SURAT.

when she was with her mistress. Jahanara, thinking only of how to save the poor girl, tried to put out the flames, and was badly burned. She was very beautiful, and the Emperor was miserable at the thought that she might be disfigured for life.

Then he heard that at the English factory in Surat, there was a very clever doctor, and he sent word to him to come to Court at once.

Dr. Gabriel Boughton obeyed, and succeeded in curing the Princess, so that she was as beautiful as ever. The Emperor was delighted, and told him to name his own reward; would he have gold or jewels? would he have lands, or a place at Court?

The doctor answered, "I would have leave from Your Majesty for the Company to trade in Bengal, free of all duties, from this time forth."

The Emperor gave leave at once, and the good doctor went away having done much for his country and nothing for himself, like many Englishmen who laid the foundations of our Empire.

Some historians say that it was not the Princess Jahanara whom Dr. Boughton cured, but another lady in the palace. However it was, the Company had leave to build a factory in Bengal, and they chose a place on the banks of the river Hughli.

Some time afterwards, the Emperor Farrukh-siyar was taken ill. He was a weak and foolish man, unfit to rule, but his name is worth remembering because, finding that none of his own doctors could cure him, he asked the Company for a surgeon. William Hamilton, who

FARRUKH-SIYAR.

was sent to him, was such another man as Gabriel Boughton. He cured the Emperor, and when told to name his fee, asked for a grant of lands for the Company.

He obtained some villages near Madras, and lands extending for ten miles on either bank of the Hughli. Then the English began to build what is now the city of Calcutta.

27. THE COMING OF NADIR SHAH.

After the death of the Emperor Aurangzib, the Empire of Delhi went to pieces. The Moghuls had become soft and unwarlike, after living for several generations in the hot climate of India. They gave themselves up to luxury, and forgot how to fight. If they could not keep their empire with the sword, they were bound to lose it.

There were enemies all round them; the Rajputs and the Marathas were always at war with the Moghuls; and the Sikhs, of whom you shall hear more, by-and-bye, were becoming dangerous. A strong wise emperor might have done something to put off the ruin of Delhi, but nearly all the emperors who came after Aurangzib were weak and foolish.

The great nobles of Delhi, such as the Nizam of Hyderabad, and the

NADIR SHAH.

Viceroy of Oudh, whose fathers had fought for the Empire, now quarrelled with each other, and seized the opportunity to set up independent kingdoms for themselves.

One of the most terrible blows that ever has fallen upon Delhi, was the invasion of Nadir Shah, at the time when King George II. was reigning in England.

Nadir was a Turkoman slave, who rose to be a general, and then made himself Shah of Persia. When the news came that he had crossed the Indus, and was on his way to Lahore, the Court of Delhi was terror-stricken. The generals, instead of fighting against him with all their might, quarrelled among themselves. The Emperor Mohammad Shah was such a poor creature that he came out to the Persian camp, and agreed to pay a large sum of money, if Nadir and his army would go quietly home. Nadir consented, but insisted that his men must first have a few days' rest in Delhi.

So Nadir and the Emperor went side by side into Delhi. Nadir, who rode on horseback, was over six feet high, with a hooked nose, a thick black beard, and a face burned brown by exposure to all weathers. Mohammad, who reclined on the back of an elephant, was a heavy-looking man, with hanging cheeks and stupid staring eyes.

The people of Delhi were terribly frightened but Nadir kept his army in such stern order that for two days no harm was done.

28. THE SACK OF DELHI.

No one knows exactly what happened in the middle of one night to give the alarm that Nadir had been assassinated by Mohammad's orders. It was quite untrue, but on hearing it, the people of Delhi lost their heads and fell upon the Persians. Then Nadir, hearing that some of his men had been killed, gave orders for the massacre of the people of Delhi.

For nine hours, he sat on the roof of a mosque, watching his soldiers kill the citizens and set fire to the houses. Then Mohammad plucked up courage to approach him. "What would you? Speak!" thundered Nadir.

Mohammad burst into tears, and cried, "Have mercy on my unhappy people!"

THE GOLDEN MOSQUE

FROM WHERE NADIR SHAH WATCHED THE MASSACRE.

Nadir, relenting, stopped the massacre, but as soon as he had ceased from killing, he began to plunder. When he had taken all the jewels and gold that he pleased, his soldiers were allowed to help themselves to all they could get. Those of the miserable people of Delhi who had been left alive, were stripped of all their possessions.

They must have been thankful to see the last of Nadir, even though he carried away with him the wealth of Delhi, and all the most skilled workmen and artisans in the city.

As a parting present, he obliged Mohammad to give him the Peacock Throne.

But there was one precious thing which he had not been able to lay hands on, and that was the great diamond which used to hang down from the pearl fringes of the canopy. It was there no longer, and no one knew what had become of it.

At last a woman of the palace betrayed to him that the diamond was hidden in a fold of Mohammad's turban.

When Nadir was taking leave, he embraced the Emperor. "We are brothers now," he said, "and in token of it, let us exchange turbans."

Mohammad knew this meant that his secret had been found out, but there was no help for it. He let Nadir's turban be placed upon his head, and gave up his own.

Nadir thrust his fingers into Mohammad's turban, and drew forth the diamond. As he held it up, it gleamed so brightly that he exclaimed "Koh-i-Nur!" ("Mountain of light!") by which name it has been known from then till now.

Nadir and his army went back to Persia. The diamond brought him no luck. He grew almost mad with cruelty and jealousy, and was assassinated by some of his followers whom he had meant to kill.

We do not know what became of the Peacock Throne. It is said not to be in the Persian Treasury; probably, it was broken up by some later Shah of Persia. As for the great diamond, after many more adventures it came to England, and you may see it in the Tower of London.

The Emperor Mohammad lived to see India invaded again—this time, by the Afghans—and died of a broken heart, having been reduced to such poverty that he was buried in an old clock-case, instead of a coffin.

29. GURU NANAK AND GURU ARJUN.

While England was distracted with the Wars of the Roses, a grain merchant and his wife in Lahore were much grieved over the behaviour of their son, Nanak.

He was a troublesome boy who, when he was sent out to work, idled away his time. It was useless even to send him out with the buffaloes; he would let them stray where they pleased, while he dreamed with his eyes open.

GURU NANAK.

But it was not stupidity or laziness that made Nanak behave in this way.

He was thinking of God, and trying to find Him. He went to Hindu teachers, but their religion, with much that was beautiful had much that was cruel and

BUDDHA TEMPLE, GAYA,
VISITED BY NANAK IN HIS PILGRIMAGE TO HOLY PLACES.

disgusting, and they were tied by their rules of caste that separated one man from another. He went to Muslims, but their religion did not satisfy him. He made pilgrimage to holy places all over India, through Persia, as far as Mecca; and the people began to revere him as a saint. Then he taught them what had been borne in upon him. "God is One, and before Him race and caste are nothing. He will not ask to what race a man belongs; He will ask what he has done."

Both Hindus and Muslims were among Nanak's followers, whom he called Sikhs (disciples). When he died, one of them succeeded him as "Guru," or teacher.

For some time, the Sikhs were poor, and few in number. They began to increase in numbers and importance under the Guru Arjun, whose father, another Guru, had been granted a piece of land to the north of Lahore by the Emperor Akbar, who liked to hear him talk of religion. On this piece of land the Sikhs made a tank, in the midst of which now stands the Golden Temple, their holy place. Round the Temple, they built the city of Amritsar. Arjun collected the writings of Nanak, and made them into a book called "the Granth" which is kept in the Temple.

THE GOLDEN TEMPLE, AMRITSAR.

For many years, the Guru Arjun had no children. His wife heard that one of Nanak's disciples, a very holy man, was still alive, and went to him, to beg him to pray that she might have a son. She wore a rich *sari*, and a train of servants followed her, who bore offerings fit for a queen to give. But the old man turned away his head, and said no word to her.

She went away, weeping. Then she came again, without any servants, dressed as a peasant, with bare feet. The only offering she brought was a dish of coarse food, such as the poorest eat. Then the holy man smiled. "You shall have a son, and from him shall descend all the Gurus who are yet to come." Then, picking a handful of onions from the dish, he said, "As I crush these onions, so shall your son crush the heads of his enemies."

The prophecy came true; Arjun's son was born, and was the first of the Gurus to train the Sikhs for war, and lead them against their enemies.

30. GURU TEG BAHADUR AND GURU GOBIND.

Arjun's grandson, Teg Bahadur, was one of the most renowned of the Gurus. The Sikh stories say that he was a very good man; other stories say that he robbed the rich, in order to give their money to the poor, like Robin Hood in England. The Emperor Aurangzib was displeased with him, either because of his religion or because of his robberies, and ordered him to come to Delhi to answer the accusations against him. Teg Bahadur durst not disobey, although he knew that he was going to his death. When he reached Delhi, he was thrown into prison.

After he had lain there for some time, he was taken before the Emperor, who condemned him to death, because when allowed to walk on the prison roof, he had presumed to gaze at the rooms of the ladies of the palace.

"O Emperor!" cried the Guru, "I looked not towards your palace or your queens! I looked towards the white men from overseas, who shall destroy your empire!"

the Punjab, sometimes they were scattered by the imperial troops, and obliged to skulk among the hills and jungles.

RANJIT SINGH.

When Gobind died, there was no other Guru to succeed him, but the Sikhs have had many leaders in battle. When the Empire of Delhi was torn to pieces by Nadir Shah, Ahmad Shah, and other invaders, the Sikhs had their opportunity and conquered a great part of the Punjab for themselves.

Later on, in the time of the Maratha wars, a Sikh chieftain named Ranjit Singh made himself head of all the Sikh clans and Maharaja of Lahore. He was a wise man, and became the ally of the English ; but the son who came after him was foolish, and the kingdom soon fell to pieces.

HINDU TEMPLE CONVERTED INTO MOSQUE.

PART VI.

THE DOWNFALL OF THE MOGHUL EMPIRE.

STORIES OF ROBERT CLIVE.

31. THE FRENCH AND THE ENGLISH.
32. THE DEFENCE OF ARCOT.
33. THE VICTORY OF PLASSEY.
    (BATTLE OF PLASSEY, 1757.)

34. THE STORY OF THE TIGER FORT.

35. THE LAST BATTLE OF PANIPAT, 1761.

STORIES OF THE MYSORE WAR.

36. THE PRISONERS OF HAIDAR ALI.
37. THE FALL OF SERINGAPATAM.
    (SERINGAPATAM STORMED, 1799.)

38. THE LAST SACK OF DELHI.
39. THE FATE OF GHULAM KADIR.
40. THE LAST EMPERORS OF DELHI.
    (BATTLE OF ASSAYE, AND BATTLE OF DELHI, 1803.)

EAST INDIA HOUSE,

THE HEADQUARTERS OF THE EAST INDIA COMPANY IN LONDON.

31. THE FRENCH AND THE ENGLISH.

Two hundred years ago, there was no master over all India. The Emperors of Delhi were feeble creatures, who did not know how to rule what little part of their empire was left to them. Some of the great vassals of Delhi, such as the Nawab of Bengal, and the Nizam of the Deccan, though they pretended to govern in the Emperor's name, were independent of him, but no one was strong enough to force all the rest to obey. Persian and Afghan invaders came down from the North, and carried back the treasures of India to their homes, but none of them set up an empire in India.

If India ever were to be peaceful and prosperous, some power must arise that could make all the princes and chieftains cease fighting with each other, and keep away invaders. For some time it seemed as if the French would be the men to do this.

A great French Minister, Colbert, in the reign of Louis XIV., founded the Compagnie des Indes Orientales, which prospered greatly, and was of far more importance in India than the English East India Company. The French Compagnie's possessions were close together, in the south of India. The East India Company had a trading station on the Hughli river in Bengal, another many miles away at Bombay, which Catharine of Braganza, the wife of Charles II., had brought as part of her dowry, and another, far away from either of them, at Fort St. David in Madras. This made it very difficult for the English to defend their stations in time of war.

When war broke out between France and England, in the reign of George II., the French and English in India fought with each other, and at first the English had much the worst of it. Their troops were commanded by stupid and incapable officers, and in a little while the French had driven them from every place in the south of India except Trichinopoly and Fort St. David. Trichinopoly was so closely besieged by the French that it could not hold out much longer. A

FORT ST. GEORGE IN MADRAS.

young Englishman, Robert Clive, had come out to Madras as a writer in the Company's service. He had been a troublesome unruly boy, at home; now that he was a tall young man of six and twenty, he was quiet and reserved, given to

ROCK FORT AND TEMPLE, TRICHINOPOLY.

sitting by himself and thinking. He thought to some purpose, for he came one day to the Governor of Fort St. David with a proposal. There was little hope of being able to drive the French from Trichinopoly, with the few men that were left to the English; but if Clive were given the command of a small force, he thought he could take Arcot, a town which the French had left almost undefended.

The Governor saw that nothing could make the English position much worse than it was, and that this plan, if it succeeded, might save them. He gave Clive the command of 200 English soldiers, 300 sepoys, and three small guns.

32. THE DEFENCE OF ARCOT.

In storm and thunder and rain, Clive reached the gates of Arcot, and finding no one to oppose him, marched in, and took possession of the fort.

The first thing he did was to order his men to touch nothing in the town; then he set them to work to repair the fortifications. The Nawab of Arcot, hearing what had happened, sent 4000 of his best troops to turn the English out of the fort. The English would not be turned out, although the Nawab's guns made a breach in the walls. Clive's guns were very small, but he found in the

ROBERT CLIVE.

fort a huge cannon which had been cast long ago for the Emperor Aurangzib, and his men dragged it to the top of a tower, and fired it once a day upon the enemy, until it burst in pieces at the fourth discharge.

GUN CALLED MALIK-I-MAIDAN,

CAST IN 1548.

Some troops sent from Madras to Clive's help, were beaten back. Provisions in the fort began to run low, and all the men had to be put upon short rations. One day, the sepoys came to Clive, and said they would be satisfied with the water in which the rice had been boiled, if he would give the whole ration of rice to their English comrades, who needed solid food.

After the siege had lasted for over six weeks, the Nawab's son burst open the gates with elephants, there was a fierce fight, hand to hand, for some hours, and then he was driven back, leaving hundreds of his men dead about the walls. Next day, he broke up his camp, and marched away, giving up all hope of taking Arcot.

Clive at once led his men in pursuit, and overtook him on the banks of the river Arni. Though by this time the Nawab's army had been strengthened by some French troops, Clive gave them a good beating. They were obliged to retreat, and leave their guns behind them.

It was at Arcot that the Indian sepoys first learned to trust their English officers; and it was Arcot that first showed them how the English can turn round upon their enemies, and win a victory, when they seem to have been thoroughly beaten.

After this, Clive won many victories over the French, who at last were obliged to make peace upon terms that the English decided.

33. THE VICTORY OF PLASSEY.

Some time after this, Calcutta was attacked by Siraj-ud-daula, the Nawab

SIRAJ-UD-DAULA.

of Bengal, who believed that the English had great stores of wealth in the fort.

He was a cruel prince, who used to amuse himself by killing and torturing his own subjects, and robbed them without mercy. He now thought that he would rob the English.

BLACK HOLE" MONUMENT

Sad to say; the Governor and Commandant of the fort did not behave like Englishmen, but made their escape, leaving the garrison to the mercy of Siraj-ud-daula, who was known to hate the English.

There was a civilian, Mr. Holwell, in the fort who did what he could to defend it. Finding that he could not keep the enemy out, he made an agreement by which the Nawab promised to spare the lives of the garrison, and of the women and children.

Siraj-ud-daula had imagined that the English were very rich. On finding very little money in the treasury, he was so furious that he shut up his English prisoners in the "Black Hole"—a little room where they suffocated all through a June night. One hundred and forty went in; only twenty-three came out, next day.

FORT WILLIAM IN BENGAL.

Then Clive came from Madras, defeated Siraj-ud-daula and took back Calcutta.

Even after this lesson, the Nawab would not leave the English alone. He was so hated that his own nobles conspired against him, and betrayed him to the English. He had no friends left and every one was glad when a year after the "Black Hole," he was again defeated by Clive, who won the battle of Plassey, one of the greatest victories of the English in India.

Deserted and robbed by his own soldiers, the Nawab fled for his life. Being recognised by a faquir whose nose and ears had been cut off by his orders, he was taken prisoner and put to death by one of his own nobles.

From this time, the English were supreme in Bengal.

34. THE TIGER FORT.

When the French and English were at war in India, the best of the French generals was the Marquis de Bussy. The people of southern India believed that no one could withstand him.

Now, about a hundred years before this time, a Rajput chieftain had come to Madras, and built a fort on land granted to him by Sher Mohammad Khan of Chicacole. "Sher" means a tiger, and in memory of the giver, the

MONUMENTAL PILLAR

ERECTED ON THE SITE OF THE FORT OF BOBBILI.

chieftain called his fort Bobbili, "the royal tiger."

His descendant, Ranga Rao, was living at Bobbili in Bussy's time; unluckily, he had fallen out with the ruler of Chicacole, whose name was Viziarama. Viziarama came to Bussy, and told many untruths, to persuade him that Ranga Rao was secretly conspiring against the French.

So Bussy came to Bobbili, and summoned the chieftain to surrender. Bussy was a wise and generous man, who well deserved the admiration that all felt for him, whether they were friends or foes. He did not make his terms hard; if the Rao would give up Bobbili, he promised him a full pardon, and a grant of lands elsewhere.

Ranga Rao was too proud to explain that he had never conspired against the French; all the answer he returned was that he would never surrender the lands that had come to him from his forefathers.

At dawn next day, Bussy turned his guns upon the mud defences of the fort; in a little while, several breaches were made, and he sent a storming party forward. But the breaches were filled by the garrison, who resisted so bravely that after four hours' hand-to-hand fighting, Bussy was obliged to recall his men, and turn on his guns again.

The breaches grew wider and wider, and once more the storming party tried to enter. Once more, after several hours' fighting, they had not gained a single foot of ground inside the fort, and were obliged to come back.

Then Bussy turned on his guns for the last time, and after wrecking the defences completely, at sunset the French marched into the fort. No one tried to stop them. All around lay the garrison, every man dead, or mortally wounded, at the side of their dead chief. The women had all slain themselves.

As the French officer in charge of the storming party looked round upon the dead, from a dark corner crept a very old man with a tiny boy in his arms. "This is the son of Ranga Rao, whom I have preserved against his father's will," he said.

The boy was taken to Bussy, who promised to care for him. Later on, when the English had overthrown the power of the French in India, they restored the boy to his father's lands, and Bobbili is held to-day by a descendant of his heir.

Three nights after the taking of Bobbili, an alarm was given in Bussy's camp.

Viziarama had been stabbed to death. The men who killed him had not tried to escape; they were followers of Ranga Rao, sworn to avenge his death. "Look here!" they said, pointing to two-and-thirty wounds on Viziarama's body; "we are satisfied." They had avenged their chief, and cared nothing that they must die for having fulfilled their vow.

35. THE LAST BATTLE OF PANIPAT.

After Nadir Shah had carried away the Peacock Throne and the Koh-i-Nur, and many other treasures, there was still spoil to be had in the empire of Delhi. The men of the North meant to have it, as in the days when Mahmud the Idol-breaker had led his army down from the hills.

After Nadir Shah's death, an Afghan chief, Ahmad Shah Durani, four times invaded India. Delhi was sacked twice, until little was left within its walls but ruins and dead bodies.

Neither the English nor the French were yet strong enough to drive out these invaders, and restore peace to India.

But the Marathas believed they could get rid of them. Since the days of Sivaji, the Marathas had become very powerful; they hated the Afghans, both

AHMAD SHAH DURANI.

as foreigners and as Muslims, and they dreamed of ruling India by a great Hindu confederacy. So they gathered a large army, and marched to Delhi; there was little booty left there, by this time,.

but rather than go empty-handed, they tore down the beautiful silver and gold ceiling which a French artist had made for the Diwan-i-Khas of Shah Jahan. Then they entrenched themselves in a fortified camp, on the great plain of Panipat.

When Ahmad Shah arrived with his army, he did not attack them; they had many guns, and he had few. He encamped at some little distance. The Marathas were safe behind their ditches and trenches, but it was not long before they began to be very hungry. Their food was running short, and they could get no more, because the Afghan cavalry rode up and down the country, preventing any one from bringing them fresh supplies. Their horses were starving, because if the grass cutters went out from the camp to get forage, the Afghans fell upon them.

At last, when they had had nothing at all to eat for two days, the Maratha leaders met in the great durbar tent, and ate up the last scraps of food. They dyed their hands and faces yellow, and left one end of their turbans hanging loose, in token that they meant to die fighting; then they poured out of the camp.

INTERIOR OF DIWAN-I-KHAS OF DELHI PALACE.

The battle lasted for many hours, and at first it seemed as if the Marathas would get the better of it. But two of their leaders turned, and left the field, and this disheartened the rest so much that they were utterly routed. Thousands of them lay dead upon the field, and thousands more were taken prisoners by the Afghans.

Ahmad Shah, although he gained the victory, had lost so many men that he could not stay in India. He went back to the North, with what was left of his army.

This was the last great battle fought on the plain of Panipat.

36. THE PRISONERS OF HAIDAR ALI.

One of the worst enemies of the English in India was Haidar Ali, a soldier of Afghan descent. In the general confusion, when the French and the English were fighting each other, he had contrived to make himself ruler of Mysore, setting aside the Raja who was its rightful sovereign.

He was a keen and brave soldier, and a cruel and oppressive ruler. His subjects went in such terror of him that they durst not speak to each other in

HAIDAR ALI.

the streets, for fear that his spies should accuse them of conspiring against him.

A Brahman in his service was discovered in a plot to depose Haidar. The Brahman was seized; some of the royal ladies in the palace pleaded for his life. "Have no fear," said Haidar, "I will cherish him as though he were my parrot." As a parrot is a favourite pet

THE FAMOUS TEMPLE AT DWARASAMUDRA (HALEBID), MYSORE.

DETAIL OF CARVINGS ON WEST SIDE.

in Muslim houses, the ladies took this to mean that the Brahman would be kindly treated. But Haidar actually shut the wretched man up in a cage, and fed him upon rice and milk and birdseed until he died.

In the reign of George III., the French were at war with the English; Haidar, who hated the English, allied himself with the French, and led an army into Madras. The President and Council of the East India Company at Madras had made no preparation for war, and did not know that Haidar was on their ground until they saw the smoke of the villages that he was burning. He surprised a detachment of English and sepoys that was marching to the help of Madras. The detachment nearly beat him off but a French officer, who was with Haidar, noted the position of the English ammunition, and fired a shot, which exploded it all. Even then, without ammunition, the English held out against thirteen charges of Haidar's force, under a terrible cannon-fire. But the sepoys could stand it no longer, and for their sake, the English Colonel was obliged to surrender.

Directly after the surrender, Tipu Sultan, Haidar's son, and his Mysore cavalry, began to murder their prisoners, both English and sepoys. If it had not been for the French officers, who insisted that the massacre should stop, not one of our men would have lived to tell the story of that day.

37. THE FALL OF SERINGAPATAM.

Those prisoners who were not killed at once, were so cruelly treated that many of them died of it. They were jolted along the roads in rough carts in the burning heat; they were given nothing to drink, nothing to bind their wounds, and were stripped almost naked. They were put into different prisons; some were sent to Seringapatam, the capital of Mysore, where they were chained, two together, each man loaded with heavy iron fetters.

Among them was a young Captain, David Baird, who had come from Scotland to fight in India; he was wounded in the head, the leg, and the arm. When the jailer came to put the irons upon him, Captain Lucas, another of the prisoner, pointed out that the wounds in Baird's leg were so bad that he would certainly die if he were fettered.

"It must be," said the jailer, "I have been given so many pairs of irons, a pair for each prisoner, and I dare not take a pair back."

"Then put two pairs on me," said Lucas. When the governor of the prison heard this story, he was so much struck by Lucas's unselfishness that he excused Baird from wearing the irons until his wound was better.

Everything was done to break the captives' spirit. They were crowded together; they were half-starved, so that all they could do was to keep themselves from snatching the food out of each other's hands. Diseases broke out amongst them, and neither doctors nor medicines were to be had. They were given no news, except that their jailers would tell them terrible stories of disasters and defeats to the English. Haidar sent word to them, over and over again, that if they would abjure their country and their faith, and enter his service, they should be taken from their miserable dungeon into a palace, and be well paid, and have as many horses, palkis, and wives as they liked. But one and all held firm, and whenever King George's birthday came round, on June 4th, they feasted upon plantains, which were all they could get to make a feast, and drank his health in sherbet.

Baird and the other officers were shut up together and there were over a hundred privates of the 73rd Highlanders in another house. These men, hearing

TIPU SAHIB.

from native servants how the officers were suffering, picked out the best part of their food, and managed to smuggle it into the officers' prison. A number of sepoys had been taken prisoners with

STORMING OF SERINGAPATAM.

the Highlanders; they were kept at hard work, and given a miserable allowance of food, yet they saved some of it for the Highlanders.

We are told that in all the misery and horror of captivity, it was beautiful to see how every man was more anxious for his fellow prisoners than for himself.

After nearly four years' imprisonment, Baird and some of the survivors were released; Lucas had died in captivity. Haidar Ali was dead, and had been succeeded by Tipu Sahib. Peace had been made between the English and the French, and it had been agreed that the prisoners on either side should be given up. But Tipu, in spite of this agreement, detained many of his prisoners, and afterwards murdered them.

It was fifteen years before Baird saw Seringapatam again, and then he came to it, not as a prisoner, but as a general leading the man who stormed it. Tipu had proved even more cruel than his father, and the English were obliged to make war upon him, in order to defend some of their allies whom he had attacked. Defeated, he shut himself up in Seringapatam, and was killed during the assault upon it.

The rightful heir to the throne of Mysore was a baby of five years old, and he was made Raja, under the protection of the English.

38. THE LAST SACK OF DELHI.

Some of the stories in Indian history are very terrible; this is one of them. It cannot be left out, but it shall be made as short as possible.

The rightful Emperor of Delhi at the time of the last battle of Panipat, was Shah Alam II. His father was murdered by his Prime Minister, the year before George III. became King of England, and Shah Alam took refuge with the English, to save himself from the same fate. There was no safety for him in Delhi, where the Marathas were at work plundering and destroying. You have heard how the Marathas were defeated at the battle of Panipat by Ahmad Shah and his Afghans. Though Ahmad Shah won the day, he lost so many men that he was obliged to return home, and he never came back to India. A few years later, the Marathas had recovered from their beating. They occupied Delhi again, and invited Shah Alam to come back and reign there, under their protection.

SHAH ALAM II.

Shah Alam had often begged the English to take him back to Delhi, and they had refused, having too many other things to do to be able to put him on his throne, and keep him there. They advised him to stay where he was, but he would not listen to them. He went to Delhi, and the Marathas enthroned him as Emperor.

His reign was a most miserable one. It would have taken a very strong man to hold his own, in those days, and Shah Alam was weak. He sat in the beautiful marble palace that Shah Jahan had built, writing verses or reading the Koran, while his officers of state plundered him, and one set of enemies after another invaded his territories. His people made a rhyme about him which said that he was "Emperor from Delhi to Palam." (Palam is a village about ten miles from Delhi.)

Shah Alam had been in Delhi for some years, when the city was entered by an Afghan, Ghulam Kadir. He pretended to come as a friend, but as soon as he had sent away the palace guards, and put his own troops in their place, he showed that he had come for plunder. He seized the Emperor's jewels; he pulled up the floors of the rooms, thinking to find treasure, and he tortured the slaves to make them tell him where it was hidden. He even ordered the royal ladies to be beaten.

It was all in vain; by this time, Delhi had been sacked by so many enemies that there was no treasure left. In his rage at finding nothing, Ghulam fell upon the poor Emperor, and blinded him with his dagger.

The rest of what Ghulam did in the palace is too dreadful to be told. Even his own men were horrified, and warned him that some dreadful punishment would come upon him.

39. THE FATE OF GHULAM KADIR.

Hearing what happened to the Emperor, the Marathas came to his help. Knowing that he was not strong enough to fight against them, Ghulam set fire to the palace, and rode away from Delhi. Luckily, the Marathas arrived in time to put it out before it had done great harm.

Ghulam shut himself up in the fort at Meerut. The Marathas besieged him there, and after some weeks, he saw that it could hold out no longer. He knew that the Marathas would show him no mercy, so he waited for a dark night, and then escaped, with a few of his followers.

As he galloped along a road bristling with thorny acacias, his horse put its foot in a hole, and fell with him. When he picked himself up, his horse was gone, his companions were gone, and he could not find the way. He stumbled along in the darkness as best he might, and at last he reached a house.

The owner of the house was a Brahman; Ghulam offered him a valuable diamond ring, in return for food and shelter.

The Brahman had lived in a village which Ghulam's men had ravaged, in former days; he had never forgotten how the houses were burned, and the villagers murdered, and the cattle driven, and he knew the face of the man who had ordered all these things to be done. So he kept Ghulam prisoner, and sent word to the Marathas that he had caught the man for whom they were looking. The Marathas put Ghulam to a fearful death.

The poor blind Emperor lived on in the palace at Delhi, making poetry. He was supposed to have a yearly sum of money for his support, but his Court complained that the Marathas who collected it, kept so much of it for themselves that he and his thirty children and their households were nearly starved.

You may still see holes in the walls of the palace, which used to be inlaid with precious stones; these stones were picked out, and sold to buy food for the Emperor.

No one knows what became of the Emperor's jewels, which Ghulam hid in the lining of his saddle. When his horse fell, on the way from Meerut, the saddle was on its back, and disappeared with it.

In the Maratha army there was a certain French officer who, just at this time, suddenly became so rich that he left India, and went back to his native land. It was always thought that he must have found Ghulam's horse straying on the road, that night, and discovered where the jewels were hidden.

40. THE LAST EMPERORS OF DELHI.

For fifteen miserable years the blind Emperor Shah Alam lived in Delhi, under the protection of the Marathas. He was no longer "Emperor from Delhi to Palam"; he was not even master within the walls of the city.

In these years, the Marathas had been growing more and more powerful. The Maratha princes now had French officers to drill and lead their armies, and

ARTHUR WELLESLEY

AFTERWARDS THE FAMOUS DUKE OF WELLINGTON.

thought themselves a match for any one. At the beginning of the 19th century, they leagued together to drive the English from India.

Two great English generals were sent against them. One of these was Arthur Wellesley, a thin man with a big nose, who had helped to take Seringapatam, a few years before. He attacked the forces of Sindhia and the Bhonsla, near the village of Assaye, and defeated them, though they were more than ten times the number of his army. Assaye was the first great victory won by Arthur Wellesley; twelve years later, when he was Duke of Wellington, he was to win his last victory at Waterloo.

A few days before the battle of Assaye, the other English general, General Lake, had got within six miles of Delhi, and camped opposite to Humayun's tomb. His men were tired, after a long march; some were cooking their dinners, others were lying about, half-dressed, when he discovered that a Maratha army under the command of a French officer was coming down upon him.

Lake determined to beat the Marathas by a trick. He ordered his cavalry to advance, and to attack, then to fall back as if they were beaten. The Marathas, exulting, pursued them. The cavalry went on retreating, gradually drawing the Marathas after them, till they were close to a jungle of very high grass. From out of the grass came Lake himself, leading his infantry, who advanced close to the Marathas, then charged. The Marathas broke and fled.

The people of Delhi, who watched from the roofs, by seven o'clock that evening saw Lake's army camping on the opposite bank of the river, close to the city.

Three days later, Lake crossed the Jumna, and marched into Delhi. This was the first time that a British army had entered the capital of the Moghul Emperors.

Lake was escorted by one of the Emperor's sons to the royal palace. The Audience Hall had changed from what it was in the days of Shah Jahan. The Peacock Throne was gone, the gold and silver ceiling was gone; there were holes in the walls where the precious stones once set in them had been torn out. A poor old man, miserably clad, was sitting under a tattered and torn canopy; this was the Emperor, and he blessed General Lake for delivering him from the Marathas, calling him "Sword of the State, Hero of the Realm, Chief of the Age."

THE LAHORE GATE, THE FORT, DELHI.

For the rest of his life, Shah Alam remained under the protection of the English. He was the last Moghul Emperor in anything except the name. His

QUEEN VICTORIA.

son who succeeded to his titles, lived on in the palace at Delhi in great discomfort, till the year in which Queen Victoria came to the throne. Then he died, leaving a son who in his turn called himself Emperor. If you want to know what became of him, and how even the title of Emperor of Delhi came to an end, you must read the history of the Indian Mutiny. This book can tell you no more.

THE THRONE OF THE LAST TITULAR EMPEROR OF INDIA.